Systems Thinki

Praise for this book

'If you think systems thinking is all waffle and hand-waving, think again. Kate Neely has pulled together a lucid and convincing account that shows how thinking in systems makes you smarter and more effective in getting water and sanitation into the hands of communities around the world. *Systems Thinking and WASH* is full of useful tools, applied to real life settings, and fleshes out a number of developmental buzzwords – resilience, adaptive management – with real practical content. A very useful book indeed.'

Dr Duncan Green, Senior Strategic Adviser, Oxfam

'*Systems thinking and WASH* lives up to its title by supporting the reader to deepen our understanding of complex systems and to reframe both the wicked and the everyday challenges in the WASH sector.'

Angela Huston, WASH Systems specialist, IRC WASH

'With interest growing in applying systems approaches to the challenges of supplying sustainable water and sanitation services, this book presents a very welcome, timely and accessible compilation of real world experiences in diverse settings. Well worth a read for anyone wondering what systems approaches are; what tools and approaches are out there; and whether and how to apply them.'

Dr Patrick Moriarty, Chief Executive Officer, IRC

Systems Thinking and WASH
Tools and case studies for a sustainable water supply

Edited by
Kate Neely

PRACTICAL ACTION
Publishing

Practical Action Publishing Ltd
27a Albert Street, Rugby, Warwickshire, CV21 2SG, UK
www.practicalactionpublishing.org

A catalogue record for this book is available from the British Library.
A catalogue record for this book has been requested from the Library of Congress.

ISBN 978-1-78853-026-2 Paperback
ISBN 978-1-78853-025-5 Hardback
ISBN 978-1-78044-749-0 eBook
ISBN 978-1-78044-748-3 Library Pdf

Citation: Neely, K. (ed.) (2019) *Systems Thinking and WASH: Tools and case studies for a sustainable water supply*, Rugby, UK, Practical Action Publishing, <http://dx.doi.org/10.3362/9781780447483>

Since 1974, Practical Action Publishing has published and disseminated books and information in support of international development work throughout the world. Practical Action Publishing is a trading name of Practical Action Publishing Ltd (Company Reg. No. 1159018), the wholly owned publishing company of Practical Action. Practical Action Publishing trades only in support of its parent charity objectives and any profits are covenanted back to Practical Action (Charity Reg. No. 247257, Group VAT Registration No. 880 9924 76).

Cover design by RCO.design
Printed in the United Kingdom

Contents

http://dx.doi.org/10.3362/9781780447483.000

Dedication

To the millions of people who deserve, but don't have, access to water that is clean and plentiful, sanitation that is accessible and dignified, or hygiene that is affordable and effective.

And to my friends, colleagues, and others who are working to change this.

Preface

Have you ever read a book that changed your life? I read Donella Meadows' *Thinking in Systems* partly because it has a rainbow-coloured slinky on the front cover and partly because someone I admired suggested it. And yes, it changed my life. It made me realize that the ability to think beyond the linear, and to bring that to our description of the world, isn't very common. Thinking in systems seems fairly natural to me. Learning to describe my world in that way, so others understand it, is a continuing journey.

This book works in several ways. First, as an introduction to systems thinking for WASH practitioners, donors, and programme managers from both government and non-government organizations. If you have heard about systems thinking and want to know how you can apply it, there are chapters that introduce tools like system dynamics, group model building, social network analysis, and social-ecological resilience thinking. There are other chapters that describe how practitioners use these and other systems thinking frameworks in planning, monitoring, and learning from WASH programmes. There are case studies that will take you to Cambodia, Tanzania, Uganda, Nicaragua, El Salvador, Timor-Leste, Ghana, Tajikistan, Bolivia, and Vanuatu, giving you a taste of the contexts in which systems thinking is being used.

Second, this book gives us a common language that we can use to discuss and describe systems thinking, while it shows us the similarities and differences in the contexts of WASH across the globe. There are themes that occur repeatedly in the book: relationships, the importance of lived experiences, the need for diversity of voices, the need for diversity of approaches, the sometimes overwhelming complexity of social-political-economic-ecological systems, and the need to make mistakes and learn from them, to be honest and willing to learn from each other.

Third, this book gives us cause for optimism. When I called for abstracts for this book there was an overwhelming silence – no one feels like an expert in this area. It's new and a bit confusing and we are all trying to get a grip on it, like holding on to a bag full of snakes. This book is a collaborative effort to share what we know, what we suspect, and most of all, where we have been on our journeys with systems thinking. The authors and reviewers are all passionate about the ability of systems thinking to inform WASH practice and theory. It feels like a new way to think about doing development. If we can move away from technocratic, neo-liberal subjectivities, find the space to be genuinely inclusive and participatory, and shift power and share knowledge, perhaps we can find ways to meet the Sustainable Development Goals.

Finally, I hope that when you read this book it inspires you to ask questions. I hope that you question what you know and the assumptions that you make every day about how development works. I hope that you wonder if it is all too hard and complex. And I hope that in the end you realize that real change only happens when we all work together across the boundaries in this messy, complex, and interconnected world.

Acknowledgements

This existence of this book owes a lot to a lot of people. Aside from the astounding authors who have contributed chapters, and those that they have acknowledged within their chapters, we have had a stellar group of practitioners and researchers who have given advice and ideas and reviewed chapters throughout the process. The potential to forget someone makes listing this group a seriously frightening consideration but here goes... (in no particular order) many, many thanks to all of you who are striving to make this world a better place:

- Michelle Whalen;
- Alan Reade and colleagues;
- Esther Shaylor;
- Dani Barrington;
- J. Dumpert;
- David Schwab-Jones;
- Bilqis Hoque;
- Jeff Walters;
- Joanne Beale;
- Dierdre Casella;
- Christiana Smyrilli;
- Kathryn Harries;
- Teh Tai Ring;
- Rebecca Sindall;
- Paul Hutchings;
- Richard Carter;
- Therese Tam;
- Stephen Saunders.

The University of Melbourne has also given generous support to this project through grants that have made it possible to meet and work together through the process.

I also am highly indebted to the multitalented Rebecca Smyth whose ability to tell the difference between practise and practice has made quite a difference to both this book and my continued equanimity. And I would also like to thank the rather patient Clare Tawney for her enthusiasm, encouragement, and timely nudges.

About the editor

Kate Neely is a WASH researcher and systems thinker. She believes that toddlers shouldn't be dying from preventable waterborne diseases. Kate uses systems thinking to try to understand why this still happens and to try to prevent it from happening again. Kate has a PhD in WASH and Systems Thinking from Deakin University, Australia.

Acronyms and abbreviations

BoQ	bill of quantities
CAS	complex adaptive system
CAWST	Centre for Affordable Water and Sanitation Technology
CBM	community-based maintenance
CDMT	central data management team
CLD	causal loop diagram
CMO	community management organization
COWSO	community owned water supply organizations
CSI	comparative static indicator
CSO	civil society organization
DC	drilling contractors
DED	district executive director
DFID	Department for International Development
D/I	drilling/installation
DWE	district water engineer
DWO	district water offices
ET	evaluation team
GMB	group model building
HPB	handpump-borehole
HQ	high quality
HQRF	hygiene, water quality, reliable functionality (of both piped supply infrastructure and hand-pumps), and financial accountability
HPMA	Hand Pump Mechanics Association
IA	implementing agency
INGO	international non-governmental organization
K&L	knowledge and learning
LGA	local government authority
M&E	monitoring and evaluation
MoWI	Ministry of Water and Irrigation
MWE	Ministry of Water and Environment
NGO	non-governmental organization
O&M	operations and maintenance
PbR	payments by results
PM	project manager
PORALG	President's Office Regional Administration and Local Government

RAS   Regional Administrative Secretary
RWSD   Rural Water Supply Directorate
RWSN   Rural Water Supply Network
SDG   Sustainable Development Goal
SES   social-ecological system
SNA   social network analysis
SP   service provider
SNV   Stichting Nederlandse Vrijwilligers
SuSanA   Sustainable Sanitation Alliance
USAID   United States Agency for International Development
VEO   village executive officer
WASH   water sanitation and hygiene
WEO   ward executive officer
WSC   water and sanitation committee

CHAPTER 1

Introduction: WASH projects and complex adaptive systems

Kate Neely

Abstract

This chapter introduces ideas from complexity sciences as a foundation for systems thinking. It develops ideas around non-linearity and the patterns of behaviour that form the physical and social structures that exist within our society. Examples are drawn from WASH and other areas in order to highlight the practical uses of systems thinking and the pervasiveness of complexity in our lives.

Keywords: WASH, systems thinking, complex adaptive systems

THIS CHAPTER IS WRITTEN as a bit of 'primer' on systems thinking with examples from the WASH sector. If you already know enough about systems thinking and complex adaptive systems then feel free to skip this chapter and get into the case studies and other exciting chapters that follow. You can always come back to this one if you have questions. On the other hand, if you have heard about systems thinking and you aren't really sure that you understand what it is all about, then find a comfy chair, and a cup of tea maybe, and take the time to read through this chapter. If you want more information on the theory and tools, or if you prefer a multimedia approach to learning, other introductory resources are listed in the chapter 'Resources for systems thinking' (Neely, 2019).

We all know that improvements in access to and use of water, sanitation, and hygiene are incredibly important as a basis for better health and economic opportunities in developing countries. We also understand that hygiene, sanitation, and access to water supply have synergistic effects – if water is clean, close, and plentiful, and toilets are appropriate and accessible, then hygiene practices improve and health outcomes are positive. Conversely, poorly constructed toilets or difficulty accessing water can have detrimental impacts on hygiene practice and health. Also, WASH programmes are not isolated entities where there is a straightforward 'best practice' that can be applied consistently and gain consistent results. WASH programmes are diverse. They happen in cities and rural areas, with and without government cooperation, and include diverse water sources – wells, pumps, springs, rainwater, etc. They can be tiny,

http://dx.doi.org/10.3362/9781780447483.001

serving just a few households, or large, serving whole informal settlements. And WASH programmes are implemented within specific social, cultural, and environmental contexts. What is acceptable in one place is not okay in another place. You won't find a silver bullet for WASH programmes in this book – there isn't one. Our hope is that by the end of the book you will be able to use systems thinking to develop WASH programmes that fit their contexts and result in more sustainable positive impacts.

Sometimes when people talk about systems thinking, it sounds like a single idea or a single specific way of doing things. The first thing to understand is that it's really not.

Systems thinking isn't a single method, tool, or discipline. It comes from a variety of traditions and is applied broadly in multi- and trans-disciplinary studies. In *Thinking in Systems* (2008), the book which changed my life, Donella Meadows introduces systems as 'a set of things – people, cells, molecules, or whatever – interconnected in such a way that they produce their own pattern of behaviour over time' (2008: 2). Systems thinking isn't just one nice neat way of doing things, and practitioners have approached this area from many perspectives and with a multitude of purposes. Ison (2008: 144) maps the origins and main aspects of the different fields of systems thinking including General Systems Theory, Cybernetics, Complexity Sciences, Interdisciplinary Systems Science, Operational Research, and System Dynamics. With this in mind, we use the term 'systems thinking' throughout this book to describe *a purposeful awareness of interconnected, interdependent systems with self-generated behaviours*. All of these ideas will become clearer as we go on.

Systems thinking approaches have come from a lot of different fields including sociology, anthropology, and engineering. The thing that these different approaches have in common is that they all strive to find a way to deal with complexity, to understand, manage, or simply navigate the interconnected world around us. Now we need to look at Complex Adaptive Systems (CAS) theory to start to understand the interconnectedness and interdependence that we see in our natural and social world.

Complex adaptive systems theory

Let's start with a little history and context. CAS theory as an identifiable field of study and research has developed over a quite recent timeframe. The need to use transdisciplinary methods to comprehend the 'wicked problems' facing society led to the founding and proliferation of organizations like the Santa Fe Institute, which would:

> ...bring the tools of physics, computation, and biology to bear on the social sciences, reject departmental and disciplinary stovepipes, attract top intellects from many fields, and seek insights that were useful for both science and society (German, 2015).

Currently CAS theory is being applied within the social sciences, business, marketing, and economics to enable a non-linear understanding of social and ecological phenomena (Byrne, 1998). The ideas within CAS theory point us towards developing a network understanding of our world. This varies greatly from traditional views in many fields, particularly the physical sciences, where the assumptions of linearity and divisibility are at odds with the reality of an intricate connectedness within and between social, biological, and ecological worlds (Gell-Mann, 1996).

Walter Buckley recognized sociocultural systems as non-linear, non-homeostatic, and non-equilibrium systems. He believed that our understanding of individuals and society would be enhanced by an ability to incorporate systems thinking across fields that remained traditionally separate, particularly anthropology, sociology, and psychology (Buckley, 1968, republished in Schwandt and Goldstein, 2008). While tracing the history of 'feedback' thinking in the social sciences, Richardson (1999: 2) noted that 'the loop concept underlying feedback and circular causality is one of the most profound and most penetrating fundamentals in all social science'. From this, and my own observations of the convergence of ideas across different fields, it seems that systems thinking has existed in many disciplines for a long time, though a diverse range of language has been used to describe it. Once you look for systems thinking, you might find that you can see it everywhere. Certainly once you start thinking in systems you will see them everywhere.

Foundations of CAS theory

Linear and non-linear systems. In general, we have an intuitive understanding of a system as being a collection of parts that work together as a whole. The parts we are thinking of may be mechanical, social groups, or individuals (people or other organisms), or they could be sub-systems that are part of a larger system.

Because we are constantly immersed in systems, it would seem logical to have a mental model of the world that depicts it in a systemic way. Oddly, we don't. Historically, the success of the sciences in understanding our world by looking at smaller and smaller parts of it has led us to thinking that it is possible to understand the world this way. Sometimes this works, but in many cases when we study something in a laboratory we lose the context that tells us how it reacts to and changes its environment. This is why a water supply designed to serve a particular community may look great on paper but barely work at all when it is implemented. The context in a community is a lot more messy and interesting than we imagine when we are sitting in an office wondering how many taps we need for 35 households.

Complexity. This book will talk a lot about systems thinking and CAS theory so it is worth spending some time on definitions. The Oxford Dictionary (online version) defines 'complex' as 'The state or quality of being intricate or

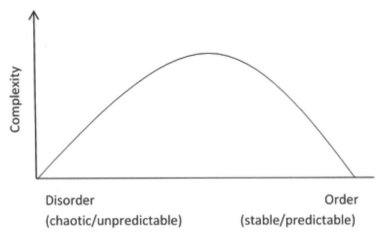

Figure 1.1 Relationship between complexity and order
Source: Parrott (2012)

complicated'. In common use the word 'complex' is equivalent to using the word 'complicated'.

However, within the scope of CAS theory, the words 'complex' and 'complexity' are both used to describe the same very specific state. The best way to understand this state is by comparing it with the alternative possible states. If we consider that a system may be either ordered, complex, or disordered (chaotic) then we would define complexity as a state that is not entirely ordered and predictable but which has some pattern to it. In Figure 1.1 it can be seen that an ordered system is quite predictable and very stable, whereas a disordered or chaotic system is entirely unpredictable and unpatterned. The peak of complexity is found between these extremes.

Systems composed of elements that are interrelated and show interdependencies that have broad patterns but limited specific predictabilities are complex adaptive systems.

For example, consider the state of various ecosystems. An intensively farmed field of wheat may be considered to be very ordered and predictable since we know from one row to the next what we will find (more wheat). Now imagine a field where the farmer has randomly introduced new and exotic plants each year, and randomly dug up sections over several years. If we walk through the field we will find mature plants and young plants, lots of different types of plants and weeds and all in a quite unpredictable fashion. This field would be chaotic as the constant random perturbation by the farmer does not allow for a level of stability or iteration to occur within the system.

In contrast to these two examples, a rainforest ecosystem is complex. We can predict the growth of canopy trees and undergrowth, we can understand the pattern of sizes and shapes of plants that occur and their response to changes in weather, but we can't predict when a tree will fall, or precisely what will replace it. Some of these factors depend on chance occurrences, wind-blown seeds, weather, etc., so there are patterns, but we need to look at several levels of the landscape and ecosystem to identify and understand them. This means that we can model how a rainforest works in general but we can't predict with any long-term accuracy what will occur at a specific time or place.

Complexity is a state where there are patterns that are not immediately obvious, because the way that they are repeated is not exact. Even if we struggle to define complexity, we do tend to recognize it when we see it. Rainforest ecosystems, coral reefs, planetary movement, human societies, and organizations within societies are all complex systems that we would recognize (Parrott, 2012).

In the development sector, we can see that poverty reduces people's choices and therefore creates a form of 'economic orderliness'. For example, in a village where everyone relies on subsistence farming it is possible to predict accurately what an individual does for a living. On the other hand, in high income countries it is possible to make broad predictions about the type of work carried out by residents in particular neighbourhoods – for example, the street I live on is populated almost entirely by scientists, engineers, and teachers, whereas the street my brother lives on is populated by factory workers – indicating that there is 'economic complexity' at work. Patterns of where people live are formed through proximity to particular workplaces and services, along with the cost and type of housing available.

Adaptive systems. When we consider 'adaptation' we tend to think about the suitability of an element for its environment or purpose in that environment. In terms of CAS, the interdependency of element and environment means that rather than adapting to its environment, a system adapts with its environment (Levin, 1998). The interconnectedness of systems means that co-evolution of this type is not confined to the elements of one system or environment, but also to related systems and their elements (Walby, 2007).

In the WASH sector, our theories of change often depend on the idea of co-evolution. We assume that when water is made available and easy to access in a village, other changes will follow, including better hygiene and health. We then assume that people will notice the better health outcomes along with the convenience of not carrying water, and will be committed to keeping their water supply functioning or even improving it. We also tend to assume that the co-evolutionary effects of reliable water supply will carry over into other areas, including education and nutrition, which will then feed back into other positive developments, including even better water supplies.

Descriptions of CAS

Complex adaptive systems are defined as systems that co-evolve with their environment, show self-organization and emergent properties, are non-linear in their dynamics, are sensitive to initial conditions, and show a certain level of 'stability' due to feedback processes that create homeostasis (Lyons, 2004). CAS can be understood in terms of both complexity and responsiveness. Definitions of CAS revolve around several key concepts. Ramalingam et al. (2008) define several concepts crucial to CAS theory that they then demonstrate with examples from relief and development environments. The following concepts are often used to describe CAS behaviours (Bar-Yam, 2002; Bossel, 2001; Ramalingam et al., 2008; Urry, 2003):

Agents are a heterogeneous group of individuals. CAS are made up of individual agents or elements, whether these are bacteria, people, atoms, schools, fish, or any number of other identifiable individuals. Each of the agents or elements in a system is in some way different from the others. Living organisms show dramatic diversity due to the well-known mechanisms of evolution, natural selection, and environmental influence. Human social organizations are always different from each other – the personalities and skills of the individuals who constitute them ensure that this is the case. Although we can determine the average behaviour or general patterns of the elements or people in a system, it is impossible to make long-term, precise predictions of the actual behaviour of individual agents (Page, 2011).

In a WASH context, and in other development interventions, this points to the need to recognize that while we may see similarities in what is happening across different communities, the reality is that each community and individual comes with a unique history and a unique response to what is happening around them and therefore while we can make some predictions about general outcomes of WASH programmes, we cannot predict what the outcomes will be for each individual or community.

Each agent acts within its own freedom to make decisions, interact, and adapt to its environment. Individual agents within a CAS interact with various degrees of freedom within, and externally to, the system. Freedom of interaction is a good determinant of the complexity of a system. For example, in a very repressive regime with strict governmental control of resources, there is little opportunity for individuals to explore or innovate in businesses by creating new products or strategies, so in this respect the society is more ordered than complex. When law and order break down in a society and anarchy ensues, at least temporarily the society is more disordered than complex. Eventually, the anarchic society might find itself with leaders who form coalitions to form a government. We would recognize a complex social order that has emerged from the previous anarchy. So complexity arises when there is significant freedom, limited by some rules (Bar-Yam, 2002). Within any CAS it is important to note that an individual agent may 'break the rules', effectively innovating or adapting to changes in their environment.

For WASH practitioners the insight here is that we should look for the positive deviants – individuals or communities who do something differently from the rest and accrue benefits from that (Green, 2016). If we can find local adaptations for WASH that work well, these can be trialled in other communities to see if they are transferrable, or how they can be adapted to other contexts.

The actions of the agents result in the emergence of new levels of organization. If agents are free to interact and participate within a simple set of rules, then this forms the basis for emergence of higher levels of organization. Individuals form groups, clusters, communities, and so forth. These may be human, plant, fish, bacteria, etc. The language used to describe them may vary, but the hierarchy of organizations is remarkably similar (Page, 2011). For humanity some of the outward signs of emergence across history are visible in our different institutions for the governing of countries.

In a WASH context this encourages us to look at the social structures that already exist and to question if an intervention is likely to meet resistance – not because communities actively resist intervention, but because emergent structures tend to be resilient.

Understanding CAS means looking at their different levels. CAS are often contained within one another. A common analogy for this is a set of Russian matryoshka dolls, but this is quite an unsatisfactory comparison as it doesn't account for the links between and within levels. Figure 1.2 is taken directly from Parrott (2002) and gives a succinct diagrammatic description of the interactions between organizational levels of complexity. Locally interacting components give rise to emergent, higher-level entities, whose existence, in turn, affects the behaviour of the lower-level entities.

Interconnections exist within and between groups at the same level of organization as well as between levels of organization. An individual may be part of several groups and several levels of organization. Understanding a CAS requires an understanding of the different levels of organization that relate to it (Bar-Yam, 2004). For example, understanding why bee colonies appear to be dying requires an understanding of agricultural practices, ecology of disease organisms (like the Varroa mite), nesting sites, bee anatomy, social structure within hives, and more. It cannot be assumed that there is a linear cause and effect that can be discovered and that will lead to a cure (Sumpter and Martin, 2004).

In a rural WASH context, these levels might relate to an individual's position(s) in a community or within the government. It can also relate to links between local, national, and international NGOs and their sponsors or donors. The current move within WASH sectors to form 'federations' of community management groups to share knowledge and experience is an engineered form of 'emergence' that, while probably useful, is likely to be less resilient than a naturally emergent grouping.

Each level of organization responds to feedback processes that act either to reduce change or to exacerbate change. Another notable characteristic of CAS is that

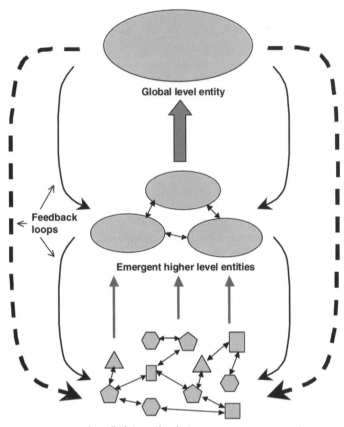

Figure 1.2 Hierarchy of organizational levels in a complex system
Source: Parrott (2012)

they may stay apparently stable through many external changes and inputs and then change relatively rapidly. This is frequently described in popular and scientific literature as a tipping point or threshold effect (Page, 2011). Tipping points are caused by unregulated effects of reinforcing feedback loops. Agents in a system, and the system itself, are subject to feedback loops.

System dynamics deals extensively with feedback loops, which can be either reinforcing or stabilizing (balancing) (Sterman, 2000). A reinforcing feedback loop will drive change in a system. A stabilizing, or balancing, feedback loop reacts against the direction of change to prevent change in a system (Sterman, 2000). Change that is driven by reinforcing feedback loops often catches people by surprise because the process is not linear and there is a widespread tendency to underestimate exponential growth or decay. In a system which also includes delays in feedback, the surprise factor can be quite large (Sterman, 1994).

For WASH, the idea of feedback loops points us towards the use of system dynamics techniques. The application of system dynamics allows us to deeply question the drivers of change or stability in a system. Does subsidizing toilets lead to more sustainable outcomes than co-investment? Does measuring NGO achievement on the basis of immediate results (toilets built) lead to sustained or unsustained change in communities? Once we understand the system dynamics we can look for leverage points to drive the system in the direction that we desire.

Change drives the process of co-evolution. Systems do not exist by themselves (Figure 1.2). Each agent within a system could potentially be a system of its own, or it could be a component of many different systems. Agents and systems can adapt to changes in their environment. As one system changes, this will drive change in associated, underlying, and umbrella systems. This process of change creating further change elsewhere is co-evolution (Byrne, 1998). One example of this is the co-evolution of disease-causing pathogens and humans. For example, each year the flu has cycles when it infects a lot of people, and some people seem to be immune to it one year but will catch it another year. This is because the virus that causes the flu is constantly evolving, which allows it to overcome human immunity (Clark, 2001). So as human immune systems adapt to recognize the flu virus, the virus evolves to become less easily recognized and then immune systems adapt again to recognize the virus and this process is iterated each year, so that each year there is a new flu virus (Clark, 2001).

From a WASH perspective, co-evolution requires us to be aware of social, policy, and physical environments that may affect efforts to implement a technical solution to water accessibility. Systems adapt with each other – as one part of an interconnected system changes so will parts of other systems – perhaps causing other changes across interconnected systems. For example, if a new water supply takes water directly from a spring, the plants below the spring may suffer from lack of water. If the plants below the spring are generally grown and harvested as a seasonal food source, this may cause people to go hungry. Adaptation to the lack of traditional plants might take the form of using more water from the spring to grow new kitchen gardens.

CAS are very sensitive to initial conditions. Edward Lorenz is credited with giving the example of the 'butterfly effect' to demonstrate how sensitivity to initial conditions works in complexity theory. The idea is that a very small action, such as a butterfly flapping its wings in a certain place and time, could determine the characteristics of a large event, like a cyclone, in a different place, several days or weeks later (De Bot et al., 2007). This example is intended to highlight the fact that in a CAS it is possible for a very small initial difference in conditions to have a very large impact on the end result (Capra, 2007). Our atmosphere and our weather are CAS. The butterfly may not create the cyclone, but its flapping wings (at a specific time and place) could cause a chain of disturbances large enough to affect the course or size of the cyclone. The settling of a snowflake in the right place, under the right conditions, could cause an avalanche.

The concept of 'path dependence' arises from the sensitivity of CAS to their initial conditions. Path dependence indicates that as CAS move away from a particular position, the next step is determined somewhat by the previous steps.

So the history of a community can often play a part in determining its response to development interventions. For example, in a year when diarrhoea has been particularly prevalent in a community, residents may be more receptive to messages about hand washing with soap. Path dependence also reminds us that every community has conditions unique to itself and so using the same approach across different communities may produce very different results.

CAS resist change (are resilient). Complex adaptive systems evolve. This means that their existence is based on a long period of growth and change. One result of evolutionary processes is built-in redundancy, so if one part of a system fails, another one will fill the niche. For example, if a programme manager in a medium-sized NGO leaves the organization, the whole organization doesn't stop functioning. The duties are passed to others and the organization continues to work with only a little adjustment required. This resistance to change in a system is also conceptualized as resilience in the sense of 'bouncing back' to a previous state or adapting to change.

> The adaptive capacity of all levels of society is constrained by the resilience of their institutions and the natural systems on which they depend. The greater their resilience, the greater is their ability to absorb shocks and perturbations and adapt to change (Berkes et al., 2003: 14).

From the development perspective, resilience, as the ability to adapt to change rather than simply 'bouncing back' to the previous state, is important, as this indicates that shocks can also be opportunities for beneficial change.

The evolutionary nature of CAS also creates a phenomenon known as 'lock-ins'. A lock-in is a situation where a system has evolved around a particular structure or social norm and despite the fact that the structure or norm may no longer be useful, it is difficult for the system to change away from it. A familiar example is the QWERTY keyboard. When typewriters were invented, the QWERTY keyboard was designed so that typists couldn't type faster than the mechanical keys could move (otherwise the keys got tangled and stuck). Although mechanical keys are no longer an issue, the inefficient QWERTY keyboard is still used by most people because changing to a different keyboard is perceived to be too difficult.

In a cultural sense the idea of lock-ins helps to explain why traditions that are either harmful or apparently unnecessary continue in communities.

From a WASH perspective, one lock-in that we might identify is open defecation (a phenomenon known for slippage) as there are many reasons that individuals use to return to 'the old ways' – comfort, fear, smell, lights, the extra work associated with maintaining a toilet. Effectively changing a 'locked-in' norm is really difficult and requires constant reinforcement or rewards. It is worth bearing in mind how difficult it would be to learn how to use a new keyboard next time we wonder why a community has gone back to open defecation – what is 'locked-in' about the behaviour and how can we help communities and individuals to see the advantage (reward) of changing this behaviour?

From a complexity perspective, both ecological and social resilience are related to a system's position within its fitness landscape or phase space as explained in the next section.

CAS are constrained by basins of attraction and phase space. This section gets a little bit scientific and is probably not absolutely necessary to know, so if you are easily scared by graphs and sci-fi looking diagrams it isn't going to hurt your understanding much if you skip to the main points at the end. Having said that, a little science might be good for you.

CAS can be described in terms of their position in phase space. Phase space is a description of all the possible states of a system at all possible times. For most real systems this is impossible to show in a diagram, as each possible state has its own dimension and it is difficult to create or understand diagrammatic representations of more than three dimensions. CAS in their phase space are constrained to a basin of attraction and they will move in a specific space around the attractor without ever returning to the same place (Capra, 2007). It is possible to predict that a system will be in a particular phase space, but not where in that phase space it will be. Figure 1.3 is a diagram of a Lorenz attractor, named after Edward Lorenz whose investigations into weather scenarios led to the previously discussed 'butterfly effect'. The diagram is a computer-generated plot of the movement of a system within an n-dimensional space. Note that the system is never in the same place twice (it does come very close), even though it follows an almost repetitive path. So a basin of attraction in development might be a tendency for the members of a community to use open defecation in preference to pit latrines, while the phase space would include every sanitation possibility, from the use of open defecation to pit latrines, composting toilets, pour-flush toilets, and even nano-membrane waterless toilets.[1]

The phase space for any CAS may contain multiple basins of attraction (different sanitation options in the previous example) scattered throughout a fitness landscape. This is shown in Figure 1.4, where the phase space can be thought of as the entire sheet and the fitness landscape is the 'geography' of the sheet. While a system exists within any single basin of attraction (stable point in the fitness landscape), it has the potential to move to a different basin of attraction. Movement from one basin of attraction to another is noticed as a threshold effect or tipping point (Urry, 2003). These tipping points tend to come as a surprise to even the most experienced observers (Sterman, 1994). While it is possible for CAS to move between basins of attraction, the tendency is to stay within the same basin of attraction. Movement between basins of attraction may be caused by large exogenous forces (e.g. an earthquake that causes a community to have an influx of development funding and

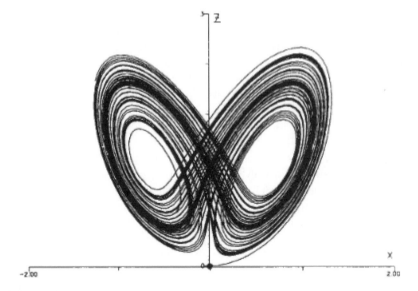

Figure 1.3 Standard Lorenz attractor
Source: Shil'nikov et al. (1993)

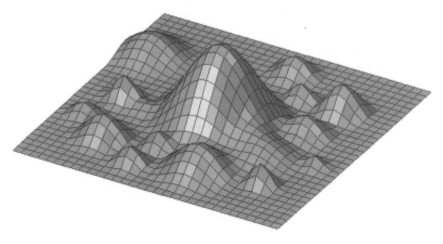

Figure 1.4 Representation of a fitness landscape
Source: Everett (2011)

professionals), small but significant exogenous forces (e.g. a prolonged media campaign), or through the effect of a changing fitness landscape (e.g. changes in government policy).

To explain this further, imagine a ball rolling around the fitness landscape shown in Figure 1.4, and imagine the ball is a small community (a CAS). That community (ball/CAS) will get stuck in certain patterns of behaviour which would correlate to the valleys (basin of attraction) in the diagram. It is difficult to change those patterns of behaviour, so the community can be said to be constrained by the basin of attraction. With critical resistance, an exogenous impact, or a change to the fitness landscape, the community might find itself moving either quite quickly or quite slowly out of a valley and towards a peak, from where it is bound to fall towards another basin of attraction (pattern of behaviour/sanitation preference).

At the point where a community (ball) is in a particular basin of attraction but appears to be moving away from it, it is useful to consider that the community isn't able to predict what the fitness landscape looks like or the pathway that will be taken. The view of the community is similar to that in Figure 1.5, where only a fraction of the landscape is known. The community might recognize that they are moving away from a basin of attraction, but they cannot know exactly where they are moving to. If the community in Figure 1.5 could see the full fitness landscape as in Figure 1.6, planning would be easier and the pathways would be known. In much of development work we make the mistake of assuming that we know or can control the pathway that a community takes, when we can only guess what the fitness landscape looks like.

Figure 1.5 Cross-sectional view of the fitness landscape from a basin of attraction
Source: Everett (2011)

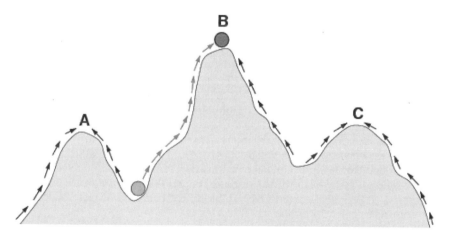

Figure 1.6 Cross-section of a fitness landscape
Source: Everett (2011)

In summary, CAS can be recognized by their limited predictability, significant interdependent links both internally and with other systems, a diversity of forms, built-in redundancy, feedback loops, emergent behaviour, and responsiveness to changes in their environment. The uncertainty that characterizes CAS is a result of the interconnected nature of the elements of the systems and the co-evolution of nested and interdependent systems to form an indecomposable whole that is robust, resilient, and adaptable.

The rest of this book will give you examples from WASH programmes of where and how systems thinking has been used, and what the outcomes have been. Some chapters will take you deeper into understanding the tools that are available and ways of applying them in your work. Keep an eye out for the boxed text as these are short comments by practitioners about their own experiences with systems thinking in the field.

Note

1. See <www.nanomembranetoilet.org/>.

References

Bar-Yam, Y. (ed.) (2002) *Complexity Rising: From Human Beings to Human Civilization, a Complexity Profile*, Encyclopedia of Life Support Systems (EOLSS), Oxford: UNESCO Publishers.

Bar-Yam, Y. (2004) *Making Things Work: Solving Complex Problems in a Complex World*, Cambridge, MA: NESCI Knowledge Press.

Berkes, F., Colding, J., and Folke, C. (eds) (2003) *Navigating Social-Ecological Systems: Building Resilience for Complexity and Change*, Cambridge, UK: Cambridge University Press.

Bossel, H. (2001) 'Assessing viability and sustainability: a systems-based approach for deriving comprehensive indicator sets', *Conservation Ecology* 5(2): art. 12 <http://dx.doi.org/10.2307/26271829>.

Byrne, D. (1998) *Complexity Theory and the Social Sciences: An Introduction*, New York, NY: Routledge.

Capra, F. (2007) 'Complexity and life', in F. Capra, A. Juarrero, P. Sotolongo, and J. van Uden (eds), *Reframing Complexity: Perspectives from the North and South*, pp. 1–26, Mansfield, MA: ISCE Publishing.

Clark, R. (2001) 'Globalization and biology: the role of co-evolution in the process of global change', *Global Change and Human Health* 2(2): 120–32 <https://doi.org/10.1023/A:1015081732376>.

De Bot, K., Lowie, W., and Verspoor, M. (2007) 'A dynamic systems theory approach to second language acquisition', *Bilingualism: Language and Cognition* 10(1): 7–21 <https://doi.org/10.1017/S1366728906002732>.

Everett, J. (2011) *Julian Everett's Weblog* [blog], <https://julianeverett.wordpress.com/> [accessed 14 January 2018].

Gell-Mann, M. (1996) 'Complexity at large', *Complexity* 1(5): 3–5.

German, J. (2015) *Something From Nothing: SFI Emerges and Synthesizes* <http://www.santafe.edu/about/history> [accessed 4 July 2018].

Green, D. (2016) *How Change Happens*, Oxford: Oxford University Press.

Ison, R. (2008) 'Systems thinking and practice for action research', in P. Reason and H. Bradbury (eds), *The SAGE Handbook of Action Research*, pp. 139–158, London: SAGE Publications.

Levin, S. (1998) 'Ecosystems and the biosphere as complex adaptive systems', *Ecosystems* 1(5): 431–6 <https://doi.org/10.1007/s100219900037>.

Lyons, M. (2004) 'Insights from complexity: organisational change and systems modelling', in M. Pidd (ed.), *Systems Modelling Theory and Practise*, pp. 21–44, Chichester, UK: John Wiley and Sons.

Meadows, D. (2008) *Thinking in Systems*, White River Junction, VT: Chelsea Green Publishing.

Neely, K. (2019) 'Resources for systems thinking', in K. Neely (ed.) *WASH and Systems Thinking*, pp. 161–168, Rugby: Practical Action Publishing.

Page, S. (2011) *Diversity and Complexity*, Princeton, NJ: Princeton University Press.

Parrott, L. (2002) 'Complexity and the limits of ecological engineering', *Transactions of the ASAE* 45(5): 1697–702 <https://doi.org/10.13031/2013.11032>.

Parrott, L. (2012) *'Measuring complexity'*, lecture delivered at the Summer School and Workshop on Complex Systems Research and Methods in Business and Biology, Heron Island, Australia.

Ramalingam, B., Jones, H., Reba, T., and Young, J. (2008) *Exploring the Science of Complexity: Ideas and Implications for Development and Humanitarian Efforts*, London: Overseas Development Institute.

Richardson, G.P. (1999) *Feedback Thought in Social Science and Systems Theory*, Waltham, MA: Pegasus Communications.

Schwandt, D. and Goldstein, J. (2008) 'Society as a complex adaptive system', *Emergence: Complexity and Organization* 10(3): 86–112.

Shil'nikov, A., Shil'nikov, L., and Turaev, D. (1993) 'Normal forms and Lorenz attractors', *International Journal of Birfurcation and Chaos* 3(5): 1123–39.

Sterman, J. (1994) 'Learning in and about complex systems', *System Dynamics Review* 10(2–3): 291–330.

Sterman, J. (2000) *Business Dynamics: Systems Thinking and Modelling for a Complex World*, Boston, MA: McGraw-Hill.

Sumpter, D. and Martin, S. (2004) 'The dynamics of virus epidemics in Varroa-infested honey bee colonies', *Journal of Animal Ecology* 73(1): 51–63 <https://doi.org/10.1111/j.1365-2656.2004.00776.x>.

Urry, J. (2003) *Global Complexity*, Cambridge, UK: Blackwell Publishing.

Walby, S. (2007) 'Complexity theory, systems theory, and multiple intersecting social inequalities', *Philosophy of the Social Sciences* 37(4): 449–70 <https://doi.org/10.1177/0048393107307663>.

About the author

Dr Kate Neely is passionate about access to clean water, sanitation, and hygiene as a foundation for development. Kate's research is framed within an understanding of complex adaptive systems and an ethos of privileging the grounded voices of lived experience. Kate is an applied sociologist with a background in science, education, and management, and she has a strange fondness for gnus.

CHAPTER 2

Systems thinking and transdisciplinarity in WASH

Kate Neely

Abstract

This chapter explores the ways in which systems thinking and transdisciplinarity intersect. In particular, we look at group model building as a transdisciplinary method for research and development. Group model building is a highly participatory method and its use with mixed groups has been effective in many areas. The application of transdisciplinary methods within development practice is suggested as a means of increasing the diversity of voices in WASH and ensuring that we hear from the residents of development focused communities.

Keywords: transdisciplinary, group model building, WASH, participatory development, diversity

ENGINEERS ARE AWESOME! Engineers have given us wells and S-bends, toilets and pumps, and pretty much all the WASH technology that we have come to rely on. At the first WASH conference I attended, the Loughborough University Water, Engineering, and Development Centre conference in Nakuru, Kenya in 2013, the highly esteemed Robert Chambers stood up in the first plenary and asked the room, 'Please raise your hand if you consider yourself to be an engineer'. Roughly 90 per cent of the room raised their hands. Given that I think engineers are amazing, it might seem odd that I was sitting there and thinking, 'Oh, maybe that's why there are so many problems with water systems.' It's not that engineers or engineering are intrinsically bad, but the lack of diversity of thinking can be a problem. Engineers are often trained to find great technical solutions in terms of functionality and cost, but rarely in terms of social acceptability. So if this conference was representative of the broader field, then there is/was very little diversity in the *approach* to problem solving used across the WASH sector. This chapter discusses ideas around the need for diverse voices to be heard in development, including the lived experience of residents of development-focused communities. I highlight some of the methods arising from systems thinking that can be used to understand WASH stakeholder groups, and to communicate effectively beyond the usual suspects. This transdisciplinary turn is consistent with taking a systems perspective of

http://dx.doi.org/10.3362/9781780447483.002

WASH, whereby we can see the broader patterns of action and behaviour in the systems we work within.

If you are reading this book you are probably on board with the idea that providing access to safely managed water and sanitation, one of the global Sustainable Development Goals, is a 'wicked problem'. This is a category of problem for which there is no easy answer, and not very much agreement on the question. It is a problem that can't be solved by linear thinking and which is different in every context in which it arises. Wicked problems are the sorts of problems that we can approach using a systems thinking perspective. When we consider community WASH to be a wicked problem, we accept that the context for each community will differ, even though the pattern of problems is similar: the lack of potable water, the need to carry water to the home, the seasonality of water points, the problems with safe storage, and the short useable lifespan of water supply infrastructure (wells, pipes, tanks, and pumps) despite 'optimal' engineering. Sanitation and hygiene show similar patterns of repetition, including, most significantly, failure to sustain behaviour change around open defecation and handwashing with soap.

Our natural (linear) response to seeing the same issue repeating itself is to assume that if we find one solution then that solution will serve in each circumstance, hence there is a drive for scaling up or working at scale across the WASH sector. But this is a wicked problem, so there is an interdependence between different areas: political, social, individual, environmental, and technical systems all act as drivers and barriers to each other, and all have different starting points. Working towards solutions in this context is likely to require diverse expertise, acknowledgement of the expertise of lived experience, and context-specific action. All of this points to WASH as a complex adaptive system (CAS).

Techniques for understanding complex adaptive systems tend to rely on working in a transdisciplinary manner. This means different disciplines and different types of organizations working together in a way that not only addresses the problem of concern, but also changes the organizations and disciplines involved (Cordell, 2010). When we introduce different ways of thinking, from sociology, chemistry, geography, local government, and residents, and have to explain our assumptions to each other, we are likely to see with new eyes the drivers of recurring issues and the barriers that prevent change (Dyball and Newell, 2015).

The idea that a lack of diversity in the WASH sector might be problematic is based in the systems thinking field of Social Network Analysis (SNA). From SNA there is an idea that we tend to unconsciously form groups and friendships where we have a lot in common. This tendency is called homophily (Wasserman and Faust, 1994). We see homophily all the time in both our private and professional lives. Think about your three best friends: do they have a common first language? Religion? Education status? Hence, we have a tendency to form thought collectives: groups of people who all think somewhat alike. Even if we don't start out thinking alike, if we work together or socialize together for long enough, we end up using similar language and having similar perspectives to those we are close to. You might notice this when a group of friends all use a common quirky phrase. In particular kinds of jobs we are often trained into a way of working and thinking. When those ways don't achieve our goals any longer, we need to break the thinking patterns that are constraining our ability to do things differently.

Social network analysis

Social network graphs show us some of the ways that homophily works against change. Tight cliques of densely connected individuals tend to share information among one another but have a tendency not to quickly incorporate new information (Wasserman and Faust, 1994). So knowledge in these cliques tends to be relatively static over long periods (think about how long it takes for change to happen in the WASH sector). Individuals who are connected *across* cliques are known as brokers. Brokers tend to have access to a broader range of information which they share across their networks. So brokerage is a good way to move knowledge and ideas into different cliques or thought collectives.

Figure 2.1 is a social network map. In the map the broker, G, sits between two cliques that are highly connected internally. By following the pathways, you can see that for information or resources to flow from one group to another it would need to flow through the broker, but once it has reached a clique it is likely to be transmitted quite efficiently. The possible exception to this is individual K who is the most isolated node in the map and is reliant on J for information or resources from within the network. Not all networks look

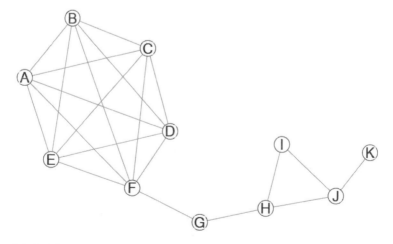

Figure 2.1 Social network map showing two cliques and a broker, G

like this and a large part of SNA is to understand what the different configurations of networks mean within their own context: being highly connected or only slightly connected isn't necessarily good or bad but will carry meaning depending on the context.

Using social networks can show us who is in a network and who isn't. A social network analysis of the WASH sector in Timor-Leste showed that, at the time of my research, there was a strongly connected group of NGO and government WASH staff based in Dili. However, the connection of this group to WASH staff in regional districts tended to be significantly less, and district WASH staff didn't form a well-connected clique. They were therefore unlikely to be sharing knowledge with each other or with the tight group in Dili. Recently, more work has been done to create WASH practitioner communities in the districts. In Cambodia, this type of disconnect is countered through the use of a closed Facebook page that is effective in encouraging knowledge sharing by WASH practitioners from different areas (Padilla and Dumpert, 2017).

Group model building

Another way to break out of the trap of thought collectives is through group model building. Group model building is a set of techniques used to enable diverse perspectives to be raised, acknowledged, and included in the process of developing an understanding of a specific problem area. Processes for group model building can include the use of toys such as figurines or plasticine for creating 3D stories, drawings for rich pictures, and system dynamics in influence diagrams (Photos 2.1 and 2.2).

Common to all of these group model building processes is the elucidation of implicit knowledge from participants, and the questioning of assumptions, traditions, and lock-ins. By using these techniques, we start to break down the communication barriers created by thought collectives including academic discipline, status, and education. Group model building achieves communication breakthroughs by creating opportunities for individuals who speak a different language (literally or metaphorically) or whose power relations are unequal, to communicate in a more visual mode and to question language and assumptions on a more equal footing. The issues of language go beyond geographical languages and play out clearly when individuals from different disciplines work together. Figure 2.2 shows how the language that we use (Person A and Person B) diverges, as the concepts that we are discussing become less concrete. At the bottom of the graph we can discuss things like 'what I had for breakfast' with very little chance of miscommunication, but as ideas become more abstract and language becomes more jargonistic in different fields, the opportunity for miscommunication grows.

For many problems, a qualitative group model building workshop can form the basis for holistic action (Newell and Proust, 2012). For other issues, group model building is the basis for further quantitative work directed at identifying specific areas for action, as shown in Box 2.1. I have facilitated

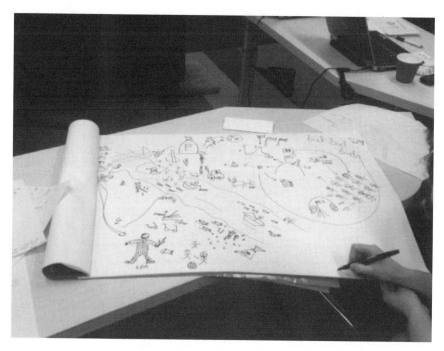

Photo 2.1 Example of a rich picture from a workshop on phosphorus shortage

Photo 2.2 Building an influence diagram for community water supply

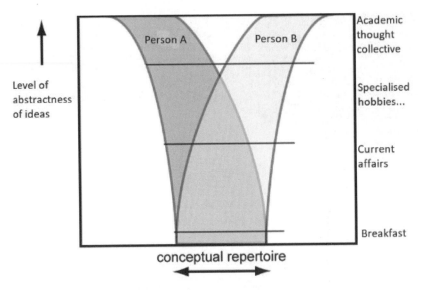

Figure 2.2 Increasing difference in language used as disciplines diverge
Source: Adapted from Newell (2012)

workshops using the process of Collaborative Conceptual Modelling developed and described by Barry Newell and Katrina Proust (2012). My workshops have involved participants from widely different areas including biologists, philosophers, engineers, and sociologists. At the end of each workshop, the debrief tends to include a level of surprise at how differently we each look at the same issues and at how using visual representations can help to overcome communication barriers, especially when questioning is encouraged. The other point brought up in most debriefs is a sense of satisfaction that all voices have been heard and treated with the same level of gravitas.

Box 2.1 Quantitative group model building in Nicaragua

An example of the use of quantitative group model building (GMB) in the WASH sector comes from Nicaragua where Walters, Pozo, and Neely were working with a group of community water committee members and leaders from the Jalapa district. This was a diverse group of people with a common interest in improving water supply across the district. The group modelling process started with brainstorming factors that affect long-term functionality of water supply in the Jalapa district. The group then reduced the number of factors through a process of clustering the factors into clearly defined key factors. The significance of the key factors was discussed and the influence of each factor on every other factor was identified and rated for strength.

From this workshop, Walters was able to develop and analyse a single influence diagram and an impact matrix, and then created a quantified order of importance of the various factors.

A follow-up workshop designed by Walters and Neely and run by Pozo presented the results of the analysis to the participants and provided space for them to review the results and consider what they might mean in terms of their own lived experiences. The participants, on seeing the results of the analysis, developed a much more nuanced understanding of the interactions of the factors. Participants noted that their initial assumptions, on day one, revolved around the importance of tariffs. But the analysis, based on their own inputs, showed that protection of water resources and engagement with government were much more important than individual payments. Discussion of these outcomes created a change in the way that the entire ecological-social-economic water system was viewed by participants. The outcome of the process was that rather than focus on payment of tariffs (which was still important), the group decided that they needed to take action in areas of environmental law, communication between committees, communication with government, and communication with water user communities.

This type of group model building, with associated analysis, allows participants to question deeply held assumptions, to re-look at what they know, and to consider knowledge from a variety of sources and perspectives. It takes us beyond our 'intuition' and looks at links across a broader system that most of us cannot see by ourselves.

Source: Jeff Walters.

One response to the increasing recognition of the need to resolve wicked problems is transdisciplinarity. Working in a transdisciplinary way involves an openness or willingness to take on board knowledge and methods from a range of other disciplines and organizations, and to allow that to change the way that you approach problems. The WASH sector is moving in this direction by taking on ideas from the fields of social enterprise, sanitation marketing, and political advocacy. By allowing the sector to be changed there is scope for new ways of doing development; likewise, there is scope for other sectors to be changed by the knowledge and practices that exist in the development sector. Group model building helps us to work in transdisciplinary teams by facilitating communication and broadening our understanding of the problem space and its interdependencies.

Participatory development

Participatory development, as another form of transdisciplinary practice, acknowledges that there are many forms of expertise: western and non-western, formal and informal, grounded, experiential, and theoretical. For NGO staff, an important transdisciplinary act is the acknowledgement that residents of development-focused communities are the experts of their own context. We can acknowledge this expertise and agency by asking questions rather than making assumptions, handing over control rather than demanding participation, and providing information based not just in engineering terms, but which discusses gender issues, health outcomes, social change, and economic impacts.

Participatory practices have been accepted as an appropriate method towards finding optimal solutions in development since Robert Chambers first asked, *Whose Reality Counts?* (Chambers, 1997). However, we need to question the degree to which current participatory practice is actually giving voice to the communities in which we work. Critiques of the use of participatory development question the level of participation or the tokenism of targeting specific groups for participation. In terms of participation, if the decision to intervene, how much to spend, and what to spend it on, all sits within rest with an NGO, then community voices have no real *power* to influence the process or the outcome of development. When communities are invited to be involved in planning processes, it is common that NGOs maintain the power to openly veto decisions, or to covertly withdraw or divert resources from community decisions that they feel are sub-optimal.

Despite their low level of actual power and decision making within a development programme, communities are often left with a sense that it is *their* fault when outcomes are short-lived, inappropriate, or inadequate. On the other hand, interviews that I conducted with residents of small communities in Timor-Leste – whose water supply infrastructures had been provided by an NGO, but later broke down – clearly indicated that despite community participation in the planning and provision of the infrastructure, they still felt that ownership and responsibility for repairs rested with the implementing NGO. In the same cases, local staff from the NGO were adamant that they had handed over the water supply and that all responsibility rested with the community. It seemed that participatory practice didn't equate to ownership in the way that we, as development workers, often assume that it will.

In the current hierarchical structures favoured by big international NGOs (INGOs) it is also worth noting that participatory development tends to be shoehorned into programmes without any modelling of participatory processes within NGO relationships. The hierarchical relationship can be seen as being:

> INGO in developed country → INGO with local office in developing country capital city → national NGO in capital city → local implementation team (NGO/civil society organization)

We can see that instructions, money, and programming come down the chain, but there is little scope for participation in decision making going back up it. What flows back up the chain are reports. These reports are formatted to the expectation of the donor and leave little room to discuss failures, or learning from unexpected outcomes, or recommendations for better programming.

So international NGOs make decisions in very non-participatory ways, with inadequate feedback processes. Alongside this, there is an expectation that implementation staff, who aren't themselves encouraged to participate in programme design and improvement, will facilitate participatory development. On top of these expectations, implementation staff also have contractual deadlines that promote the achievement of concrete outcomes (e.g. number of toilets built) over the inclusion and participation of residents.

In one of example of 'top down' development, a western-educated aid worker realized that the staff of a local NGO were having trouble with the maths involved in designing water tanks. To resolve this, he developed a spreadsheet so that they could fill in some details and the calculations would be done for them. This isn't intrinsically bad; we all like things that make our lives easier. But it neglects the fact that the local staff would be better off in the long run if their engineering understanding and their maths skills were developed to a point where they could understand and do the calculations. Given the likelihood of each new water supply to throw up a different set of problems, relying on a spreadsheet that you don't understand isn't likely to lead to great outcomes for anyone. The spreadsheet, as an answer to a problem, is an example of 'top down' development driven by a perceived need to achieve outcomes without being adequately concerned for *processes*. It takes a single perspective, engineering efficiency, and privileges that over other perspectives – such as human development or education – that might lead to more inclusive development processes. The example in Box 2.2 shows an approach to WASH marketing that is much broader than usual.

Box 2.2 Mapping with more voices

For thousands of years, people have recognized the importance and value of maps. From a systems thinking perspective, maps are very useful visual tools to record and communicate information, and to analyse and monitor complex system relationships and interactions. Systems maps can take on many different forms, from simple sketch drawings to sophisticated interactive Geographic Information Systems (GIS) maps. The form a map takes is often guided by who intends to use the map, its ease-of-use, its flexibility, and the availability of data and resources. Systems maps are also seen as instruments of power as they give rise to a visual depiction of particular realities, which some people may see as desirable or worthy (Wood, 1992).

Maps are widely used in the WASH sector to communicate water and sanitation networks, value chains, causal links, and many other systemic relationships. Mapping is also seen as a key element in the Community-led Total Sanitation (CLTS) movement (e.g. open defecation mapping) and participatory methodologies (Chambers, 2008). In more recent years, the

WASH sector has also been actively involved in mapping social and economic exchange systems (e.g. marketing systems), which directly relate to access to and use of WASH products and services, and their impact on wellbeing (Saunders et al., 2016). For instance, Saunders et al. (2016) report a simple method for generating participatory system maps that depict and explain, from a community perspective, how a WASH exchange system operates in an informal settlement. The process involved the creation of individual household WASH system maps, which were then used to construct an overarching systems map for the entire community. A unique feature of the maps was that they were also accompanied by short narratives that not only described the key elements of the system in the form of natural language, but provided a 'voice' for people living within the system.

Source: Stephen Saunders.

Developing a transdisciplinary mindset within the WASH sector has the potential to produce better outcomes all round. As we share knowledge and insights, it becomes possible for an engineer to understand why a community might need to have a sub-optimal configuration of water points so that the older people have less distance to carry water. Or it might help sanitation staff to see how the siting of pit toilets can pollute the water table. Or it might help all of us to see that communities have agency and expertise and will make changes after an NGO leaves, so reconfigurable, adaptable water supply fittings might be better than fixed structures.

When we try to see WASH from a variety of perspectives we have the opportunity to open our eyes to the interconnected resource issues that are part of living in poverty, and that alone can help us to understand why water systems fail and why sanitation and hygiene programmes show backsliding. When we work in teams that are transdisciplinary we ask different questions and we learn more. Just consider these (fictional) responses to a (fictional) broken tap:

> **Engineer:** Was the tap quality poor?
> **Educator:** Do you know how to fix the tap?
> **Sociologist:** Do the community all agree that the tap should be fixed?
> **Health worker:** Who is affected by the lack of water?
> **Politician:** Whose responsibility is it to fix the tap?
> **Local man:** Do you know the shopkeeper so that you can get spare parts?
> **Local woman:** I am so busy, I am going to the river to collect water while you work it out.

All of these fictional responses are relevant to the fixing of the tap, but it is unlikely that any one person would ask all of them. Yet WASH really does involve issues of time, local context, responsibility, vulnerability, power, skills, and quality of materials. We all need to work together to make sure that we are asking the right questions.

Engineers *are* awesome, and so are sociologists, health workers, community residents, politicians, bureaucrats, and technicians. And all these people have knowledge to share that can contribute to sustained water supply. As WASH practitioners, managers, and researchers, our job is to make sure that we find and listen to the diverse forms of knowledge, and understand how it is all connected.

References

Chambers, R. (1997) *Whose Reality Counts?*, Rugby: Practical Action Publishing.

Chambers, R. (2008) *Revolutions in Development Inquiry*, London: Institute of Development Studies, Earthscan Publishers.

Cordell, D. (2010) *The Story of Phosphorus: Sustainability Implications of Global Phosphorus Scarcity for Food Security*, PhD thesis, University of Technology, Sydney.

Dyball, R. and Newell, B. (2015) *Understanding Human Ecology: A Systems Approach to Sustainability*, Abingdon, UK: Routledge, Taylor and Francis Group.

Newell, B. (2012) 'Simple models, powerful ideas: towards effective integrative practice', *Global Environment Change* 22(3) 776–83 <http://dx.doi.org/10.1016/j.gloenvcha.2012.03.006>.

Newell, B. and Proust, K. (2012) *Introduction to Collaborative Conceptual Modelling* [pdf], Working Paper, Canberra: ANU <https://digitalcollections.anu.edu.au/handle/1885/9386> [accessed 14 June 2018].

Padilla, A. and Dumpert, J. (2017) *'The influence of real time learning in WASH programming'*, in Proceedings of the 40th WEDC International Conference, Loughborough.

Saunders, S.G., Barrington, D.J., Sridharan, S., Meo, S., Hadwen, W., Shields, K.F., Souter, R., and Bartram, J.K. (2016) 'Addressing WaSH challenges in Pacific Island Countries: A participatory marketing systems mapping approach to empower informal settlement community action', *Habitat International* 55: 159–66 <https://doi.org/10.1016/j.habitatint.2016.03.010>.

Walters, J., Neely, K., and Pozo, K. (2017) 'Working with complexity: a participatory systems-based process for planning and evaluating rural water, sanitation and hygiene services', *Sustainability* 7(3): 426–35 <http://dx.doi.org/10.2166/washdev.2017.009>.

Wasserman, S. and Faust, K. (1994) *Social Network Analysis: Methods and Applications*, Cambridge, MA: Cambridge University Press.

Wood, D. (1992) *The Power of Maps*, New York: The Guilford Press.

About the author

Dr Kate Neely is passionate about access to clean water, sanitation, and hygiene as a foundation for development. Kate's research is framed within an understanding of complex adaptive systems and an ethos of privileging the grounded voices of lived experience. Kate is an applied sociologist with a background in science, education, and management, and she has an unusual love of warthogs.

CHAPTER 3

Using causal loop diagrams to understand handpump failure in sub-Saharan Africa

Elisabeth S. Liddle and Richard A. Fenner

Abstract

Thousands of handpumps have been installed across sub-Saharan Africa over the past four decades to improve rural water supplies. However, multiple studies have raised concerns over the extent to which these sources are providing safe and adequate quantities of water post-construction. A number of factors could be causing these problems, either directly or indirectly. Understanding the interrelated nature of these factors and their inherent complexity is crucial if handpump failures are to be avoided in the future. This chapter demonstrates how some of this complexity can be understood and effective intervention points identified through the development of a causal loop diagram (CLD). To begin, the necessary theory behind constructing a CLD is explained. A step-by-step guide to developing, interpreting, and utilizing a CLD is then provided. Within this, a CLD that looks at suitability of the price paid for the drilling/installation work and the impact of this on the quality of work conducted by drilling contractors is developed. To help demonstrate the utilization phase, a Uganda case study is presented. Overall, this chapter demonstrates how CLDs can help to develop an appreciation and awareness of the complexity that lies behind a given problem, and subsequently, how CLDs can help identify the intervention points that should become the focus if a given problem is to be prevented in the future.

Keywords: causal loop diagrams, handpump failure, quality of drilling and installation work

THOUSANDS OF HANDPUMP-BOREHOLES (subsequently referred to as handpumps) have been installed across sub-Saharan Africa over the past four decades to improve rural water supplies. However, a number of studies have raised concerns over the extent to which these sources are providing safe and adequate quantities of water post-construction (Adank et al., 2014; Bey et al., 2014; Foster, 2013; Anscombe, 2011; Hoko, 2008; Engel et al., 2005; Harvey, 2004; Sangodoyin, 1991). Bey et al. (2014), for example, found 42.3 per cent of handpumps' water to have poor colour, sediments, and/or worms, while in Zimbabwe, Hoko et al. (2009) found 38 per cent of handpumps to be dry. In many cases, people have been unable or unwilling to use the handpumps that have been installed for

http://dx.doi.org/10.3362/9781780447483.003

them and have reverted to the use of unimproved water sources (Hoko, 2008; Gleitsmann et al., 2007; Katsi et al., 2007; Haysom, 2006; Hoko and Hertle, 2006; Engel et al., 2005; Nyong and Kanaroglou, 2001). If communities are to fully benefit from investment in handpumps, post-construction failures (dry/ low-yielding handpumps and/or handpumps with water quality problems) must be prevented.

A number of academic and practice-based studies have investigated the reasons for handpump failure over the past four decades (for example, Whaley and Cleaver, 2017; Bonsor et al., 2015; Fisher et al., 2015; Walters and Javernick-Will, 2015; Adank et al., 2014; Foster, 2013; Harvey, 2004; Parry-Jones et al. 2001; Hazelton, 2000; Sara and Katz, 1998; Howe and Dixon, 1993; McPherson and McGarry, 1987). These studies show the causal factors behind handpump failure to stem from two broad areas:

- the quality of the siting and drilling/installation (D/I) work during the implementation phase; and
- the extent, quality, and oversight of operations and maintenance (O&M) post-construction, as shown in Figure 3.1.

Behind each of the factors in Figure 3.1 lies a high degree of complexity, with a range of interdependent factors acting to determine the service provided by a given handpump. Understanding this complexity and how it can be harnessed to achieve desirable outcomes is crucial if handpump failures are to be prevented in the future. This chapter demonstrates how some of this complexity can be unpacked and intervention points identified through the development of a CLD. Such an approach has value in helping draw a conscious focus on the wider system interactions that might otherwise be missed or ignored.

The chapter begins by briefly explaining what a CLD is. A step-by-step guide to developing, interpreting, and utilizing a CLD is then provided. A CLD that looks at suitability of the price paid for the D/I work and the impact of this on the quality of work conducted by drilling contractors (DCs) (Figure 3.1) is used as an example. To help demonstrate the utilization phase, a Uganda case study is presented. For many readers who have experience of working in the field, the factors and relationships shown in the CLD will be no surprise. However, the aim of this chapter is to demonstrate how CLDs can help to develop an understanding of the complexity that lies behind a given problem, and subsequently how CLDs can help identify the intervention points that should become the focus if a given problem is to be prevented in the future.

What are causal loop diagrams?

CLDs highlight and hypothesize the causal relationships, feedback loops, and time delays that exist between factors within a given system boundary (Sterman, 2000). Developing a CLD helps to improve the conceptual understanding of the system structure that underpins the problem at hand, and through doing so, enables the identification of the systemic factors that

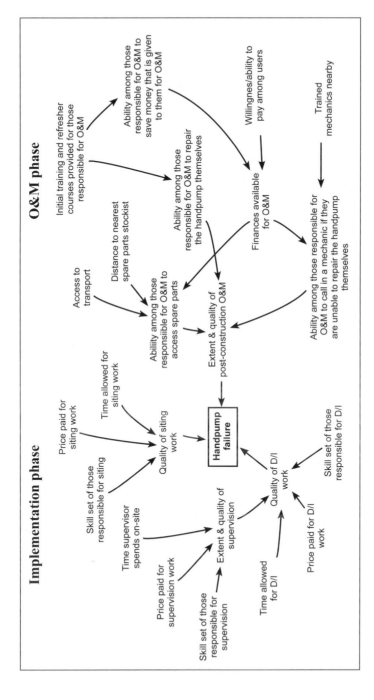

Figure 3.1 Mind map highlighting potential reasons for handpump failure from authors' point of view.

may cause certain system behaviours to accelerate or balance out over time (Wolstenholme, 2003).

In developing a CLD, one starts with the factor of interest, and then asks: 'What factor(s) affect this factor of interest?' Every time a new factor is added to the CLD, the same question is asked: 'What factor(s) affect this factor?' and so on. This process continues until the system boundary is reached. Any time delays that slow the impact of one factor on another are then added. It is at this point the feedback loops and time delays that drive our factor of interest can be observed, and hence those that need to be harnessed if the state of the factor of interest is to improve over time can be identified.

CLDs are made up of standard symbols. Arrows indicate causal relationships and dependencies between related factors. Quantitative (hard/measurable) and qualitative (soft) factors can be included in CLDs and each factor can be affected by a number of others (Maani and Cavana, 2007). Where a time delay is known to exist within a causal relationship (where the impact of one factor on another is delayed, i.e. the effect will not be felt straight away), a || is drawn onto the arrow. Arrows are then marked as positive (+) or negative (-) (Sterman, 2000). A positive sign indicates a reinforcing relationship; as one factor moves in a certain direction (increases or decreases) the other will follow in the same direction. A reinforcing relationship is noted in Figure 3.2, for example, between handpump use and handpump wear and tear: as handpump use increases, handpump wear and tear increases, or as handpump use decreases, handpump wear and tear decreases. Conversely, a negative sign indicates a balancing relationship; as one factor moves in a certain direction (increases or decreases), the other will do the opposite. A balancing relationship is noted in Figure 3.2 between handpump wear and tear and handpump reliability: as handpump wear and tear increases, handpump reliability decreases, or, as handpump wear and tear decreases, handpump reliability increases. A time delay has been added to this relationship as wear and tear will need to reach a critical threshold (build up over time) before handpump reliability decreases. The effect of wear and tear on handpump reliability will not be felt straight away. Understanding these kinds of time delay tipping points is a vital part of CLD analysis.

Feedback loops are formed when a group of causal relationships form a closed circuit. These loops are what cause dynamic behaviours to occur within systems over time (Maani and Cavana, 2007). Feedback loops may be reinforcing or balancing. A loop is reinforcing (R) if it contains an even number of negative arrows (including zero negative arrows) and balancing (B) if it contains an odd number of negative arrows. Reinforcing loops lead to self-propelling behaviour (exponential growth or decline) over time, while balancing loops lead to stability/goal seeking behaviour over time (Figure 3.3) (Sterman, 2000).

Hjorth and Bagheri (2006) refer to balancing loops as self-correcting viability loops. Two reinforcing loops and one balancing loop are shown in Figure 3.2. Reinforcing loop 2 (R2), for example, shows how an increase in handpump

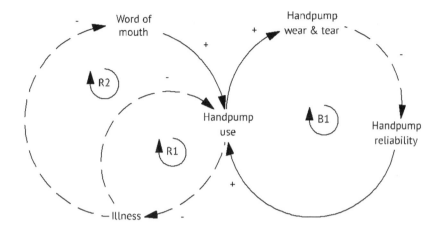

Solid lines indicate positive arrows, dashed lines indicate negative arrows.

Figure 3.2 Two reinforcing loops and one balancing loop centred on handpump use
Source: Adapted from Liddle and Fenner (2017)

use will reduce illness (assuming the water is safe for human consumption), which then leads to an increase in word of mouth concerning the effectiveness/benefits of handpump use. This then leads to increasing handpump use by additional community members. As handpump use increases, however, the balancing loop (B1) will come into effect, with increased handpump use increasing handpump wear and tear and thus decreasing handpump reliability. As reliability decreases, handpump use will begin to slow as users can no longer rely on the handpump (Figure 3.2).

The final CLD can be used in a qualitative way for assessing how changes in one part of the system may affect other parts of the system. If the loops are reinforcing loops, then exponential growth/decline of key factors over time can be expected. However, there may be related balancing loops in the same diagram that will help to control and mitigate this exponential growth/decline over time. If there are no balancing loops, it may be possible to implement an intervention to create a balancing loop, and so on.

Developing, interpreting, and using a CLD

The following sections provide an overview of CLD development, interpretation, and utilization. Figure 3.4 highlights the key steps involved in this process.

Define the factor of interest and the system boundary

Before any CLD development begins, the factor of interest and the system boundary must be defined. The factor of interest is where the CLD development will begin, while the boundary is where development will stop. Without

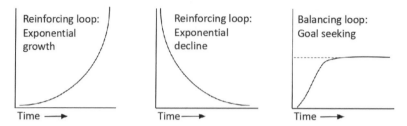

Reinforcing loops lead to exponential growth or exponential decline over time, while balancing loops lead to goal-seeking behaviour over time.

Figure 3.3 Systemic behaviour as a result of reinforcing loops and balancing loops

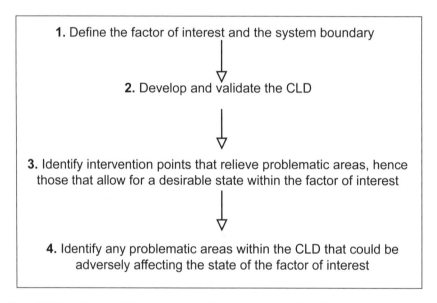

Figure 3.4 Key steps in CLD development, interpretation, and utilization

defining these aspects beforehand, the CLD will be overly complex, difficult to follow, and not fit for purpose.

Before defining the factor of interest and the system boundary, it is best to step back and ask: 'What is it that I want to understand by developing this CLD?' Mind maps are a useful tool at this stage, as they allow you to get all of your ideas down on paper, without a series of rules that need to be followed. In a mind map, the problem is placed in the middle of the page, as indicated in Figure 3.1 (the problem being 'handpump failure' in this case). Causal factors and relationships then branch off from the central problem and may be represented by words or images.

Having created a mind map, the aspect of the problem you are most interested in can be chosen. Your factor of interest and boundary will stem from this. When looking at Figure 3.1 we decided that, for the purpose of this chapter, we were interested in:

- the ways in which the price paid for the D/I work is affecting the quality of the D/I work that is being conducted by DCs in sub-Saharan Africa; and
- the higher-level factors that determine the price that is paid for the D/I work.

The factor 'suitability of D/I price paid' was therefore chosen as our factor of interest.[1]

The system boundary then needs to be defined. Where this boundary is placed is important, as the boundary determines:

- the extent to which all aspects of the system are included;
- the types of 'What if...?' scenario questions that can be asked;
- the extent to which intervention points address the root issues;
- the type and extent of knowledge needed to develop the systems model; and
- the time taken to do all of this (Sterman, 2000).

A fine balance is needed when defining the system boundary. If this is too narrow/restrictive, the CLD will not look far enough out. Our ability to understand the factors at play, and to find meaningful intervention points, will be limited. Conversely, if the boundary is too wide, the CLD will become increasingly confusing and messy, and in some cases, not fit for purpose, as intervention points will end up being outside of our control. While it is important to set a boundary before CLD development begins, it must be noted that this can be flexible during CLD development, with factors being added to and subtracted from the boundary during the development process as and when necessary.

For the CLD that is to be developed in this chapter, the system boundary has been placed, firstly, around the on-site quality of D/I work factors that the price paid for the D/I work goes on to affect, and secondly, around the implementing agency's processes and decisions that determine the price that is paid for the D/I work.[2] Figure 3.5 shows the main themes that were included in the boundary and also details the factors that fell outside the boundary.[3] At this stage, it is also important to list any assumptions that will be made when developing the CLD and the time over which any delays operate (e.g. one day, one month, one year, one project cycle) (see Figure 3.5).

Develop and validate the CLD

When developing a CLD it is best to start with the factor of interest and then work outwards from there. In the case of the CLD developed for this chapter, we firstly asked what downstream factors the factor of interest, 'suitability of D/I price paid, goes on to affect. We then moved to the upstream factors – those

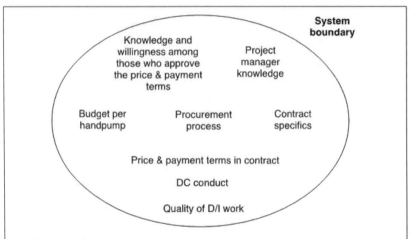

System boundary notes:

Other factors that affect quality of D/I work, for example, skill-set of those responsible for D/I, fall outside the system boundary. The factors that affect the following also fall outside the system boundary:

- the price and quality of drilling materials available in the given country;
- the quality of the site selection work and the timing of this;
- competition within the bidding process;
- corruption within the procurement process;
- whether technical staff are involved in bid evaluation;
- whether an accurate engineer's estimate is available;
- whether training opportunities are available for enhancing implementing agency knowledge;
- the extent to which implementing agencies review quality of work upon completion and monitor functionality post-construction.

Assumptions:

- A range of implementing agencies are assumed to be overseeing these handpump drilling projects in the given country.
- Each implementing agency is assumed to have a project manager who is responsible for overseeing drilling projects, as well as people above the project manager who permit and sign off on their decisions.
- D/I is assumed to be privatised, i.e. a DC needs to be procured. Competitive open bidding is assumed to be used for procuring DCs.
- It is assumed that the findings from reviews and monitoring (if conducted) are passed on to all necessary actors, including the project manager and those who permit and sign off on the project manager's decisions.

NB: The time period implied by delay symbols is one project cycle for the given implementing agency. i.e. time delays and feedback loops work over multiple project cycles.

Figure 3.5 System boundary for the price paid CLD and assumptions made

that determine the 'suitability of D/I price paid'. Every time a new factor was added, the question, 'What is this factor dependent on?' was asked, with new factors being added until the system boundary was reached. It is within these upstream factors that intervention points for increasing the 'suitability of D/I price paid' will be found. The different parts of the CLD are presented in the following sections.

A range of information sources can be used to aid the CLD development process including textbooks, academic and practice-based articles, expert and stakeholder knowledge (holding one-on-one drawing sessions or group workshops is very useful), and knowledge gained from the field. It is important that a range of sources, experts, and stakeholders are consulted during the CLD development process and that multiple disciplines are accounted for. If the scope of those involved is too narrow, important factors may be overlooked.

Once an initial version of the CLD has been prepared, it needs to be validated by those who understand the system, for example by experts and key stakeholders. From validation, iterations will be needed, and a second round of validation may be necessary. It is important to note here that CLD development is an iterative process; the first draft will very rarely be the final version. Developing an accurate CLD is no quick and easy task; it takes time and knowledge of the system at hand and cannot be successfully completed in an afternoon.

Developing the D/I price paid CLD
Figure 3.6 provides a structural overview of the 'suitability of D/I price paid' CLD, highlighting the three sub-systems and several connections between these. The factors, dependencies, and feedback loops within each of these sub-systems are described below. The full CLD (all sub-systems merged) is then presented. The following acronyms are used in the D/I price paid CLD:

- PM: project manager;
- DC: drilling contractor;
- D/I: drilling/installation;
- HPB: handpump-borehole;
- HQ: high-quality;
- IA: implementing agency;
- BoQ: bill of quantities.

D/I tasks sub-system. The D/I tasks sub-system highlights the downstream factors that 'suitability of D/I price paid' goes on to affect, with these downstream factors ultimately affecting the 'quality of D/I work', and thus, 'handpump functionality'. As noted in Figure 3.7, the downstream factors include:

- 'hydrogeological suitability of materials used and quality of these';
- 'hydrogeological suitability of borehole design';
- 'suitability of borehole development time'; and
- 'suitability of pumping test length and subsequent borehole commission decision'.

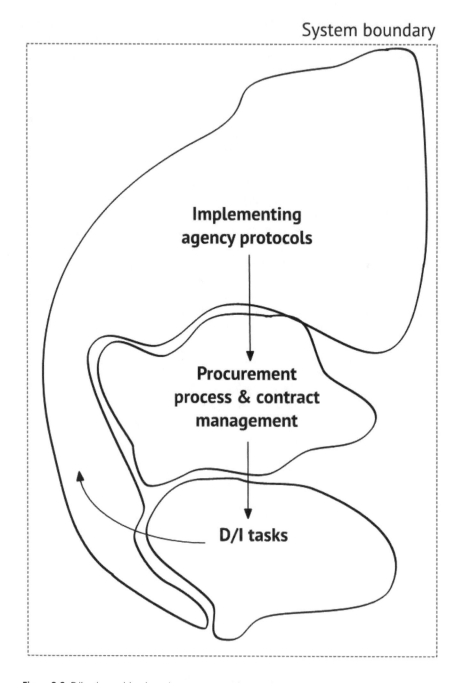

System boundary

Implementing
agency protocols

Procurement
process & contract
management

D/I tasks

Figure 3.6 D/I price paid sub-systems

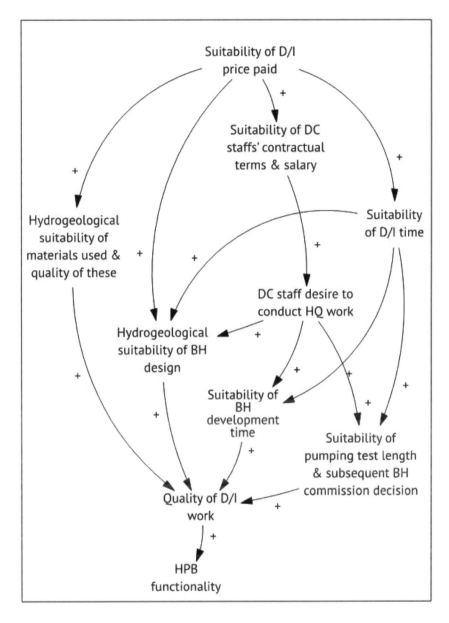

Figure 3.7 D/I tasks sub-system

All the relationships in this sub-system are reinforcing. Consequently, as 'suitability of D/I price paid' increases, so will each of these factors. There are no feedback loops or time delays within this part of the CLD.

Procurement process and contract management sub-system. The procurement process and contract management sub-system (Figure 3.8) highlights the first level of upstream factors that affect the 'suitability of D/I price paid', i.e. those that determine whether the final price the DC is paid is indeed suitable for high-quality D/I work. It is important to note here that this factor, 'suitability of D/I price paid', does not depend solely on the 'suitability of price in D/I contract', but also on the 'suitability of payment terms in D/I contract'. The DC's contract may state that they will be paid US$5,000; however, the payment terms will determine how much of this $5,000 they are actually paid. This is an important dynamic given the use of lump sum no-water-no-pay contracts in handpump drilling projects.

When looking at the 'suitability of price in D/I contract', the CLD (Figure 3.8) indicates that several additional factors, a reinforcing loop, and a time delay all need to be considered. The CLD helps to unpack some of the complexity behind this factor, some of which is explained below.

When considering the 'suitability of price in D/I contract' in Figure 3.8, we firstly realize that the 'suitability of price in D/I contract' is not simply a function of the price budgeted by the implementing agency, but rather, a function of the 'evaluation team's (ET) ability to select a DC whose price is suitable'. This assumes that under open bidding, a series of DCs bid and submit quotes. The evaluation team then selects the winning bid, with the price in the D/I contract being that which the winning DC quoted, hence, the evaluation team ultimately decides the price that will be in the DC's contract. As seen in Figure 3.8, 'evaluation team's ability to select a DC whose price is suitable' depends on:

- 'suitability of D/I quotes'
  - if DCs quote unsuitable (too low) prices, there is a risk that the evaluation team will select one of these contractors, along with their unsuitable quote;
- 'suitability of implementing agency budget'
  - if the implementing agency's budget is unsuitable, the evaluation team may be forced to select a firm whose price is unsuitable;
- 'evaluation team's awareness of price required for high-quality D/I'
  - if the evaluation team is unaware of the price needed, there is a risk that they will select a DC whose price is unsuitable;
- 'D/I procurement corruption'
  - corruption could lead to the evaluation team selecting a DC for an external reason (if for example, a bribe has been paid), rather than a DC whose price is suitable.

The factor 'suitability of D/I quotes' above raises an interesting question: 'Why would DCs willingly submit a quote that is unsuitable for high-quality

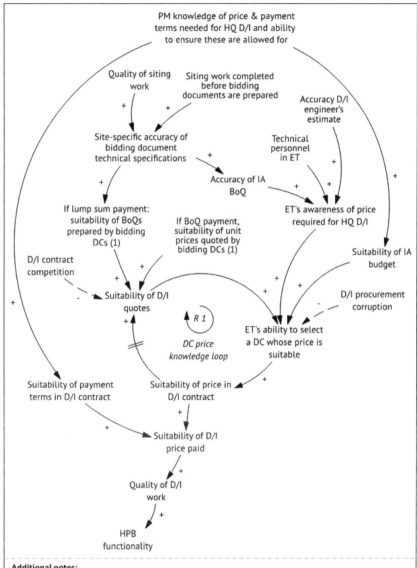

Additional notes:

(1) These two factors refer to two different payment forms – 'BoQ payment' and 'lump sum, no-water-no-pay-payment'. Under BoQ payment terms, the total price the DC is paid is based on a BoQ that is prepared upon the completion of work, with the unit prices in this being those the DC quoted during bidding. Under lump sum, no-water-no-pay-payment terms, the total price of the contract is based on a BoQ that is prepared by the given DC during bidding. The specific quantities and costs in this BoQ are based on the HPB design specified in the D/I contract bidding documents. If the HPB is deemed unsuccessful (as defined in their contract), the DC will not be paid, while, if the HPB is successful, the DC will be paid the full lump sum. Only one of these payment term factors will be relevant in a given project cycle, depending on which one the given IA is using. The other can be discounted when working through the CLD.

Solid lines indicate positive arrows, dashed lines indicate negative arrows.

Figure 3.8 Procurement process and contract management sub-system

work at the given site?' The CLD helps in explaining several reasons for this, with an important feedback loop coming into effect at this point. There is firstly the issue of 'D/I contract competition': as competition increases, the 'suitability of D/I quotes' is expected to decrease as firms attempt to outbid each other. Secondly, there is the accuracy of the information being used when DCs are calculating their quotes. This is where the factors 'if Bill of Quantities (BoQ) payment: suitability of unit prices quoted by bidding DCs' and 'if lump sum payment: suitability of BoQs prepared by bidding DCs' come into effect. Finally, there is this issue of the 'suitability of price in D/I contract' in previous project cycles (note the time delay on this relationship: this indicates that this relationship works over time, from one project cycle to the next in the case of this CLD). This relationship creates the 'DC price knowledge loop' (reinforcing loop, R1) at the centre of Figure 3.8. This reinforcing loop indicates that as the 'suitability of price in D/I contract' decreases, so will the 'suitability of D/I quotes' in future project cycles. Over time, DCs may gain an understanding of the price certain implementing agencies are willing to pay. Assuming these DCs then use these prices as their benchmark figures when bidding in the future, prices quoted may be continually driven down as DCs attempt to win the given implementing agency's contracts, with the 'suitability of price in D/I contract' then suffering. Here we see how decisions made in previous project cycles can lead to undesirable conditions and/or unintended consequences in subsequent project cycles. However, additional factors in the sub-system can help to prevent this loop from taking effect, such as an increase in 'evaluation team's awareness of price required for high-quality D/I'.

An additional aspect raised in this sub-system is the timing of the siting work in relation to D/I budget setting and DC procurement. The top left-hand corner of Figure 3.8 highlights the factors involved and their systemic impacts. Here the need for the siting work to be conducted before the DC's bidding documents are prepared is highlighted, with this affecting the 'site-specific accuracy of bidding document technical specifications'. An increase or decrease in this factor will then cascade throughout the sub-system, and ultimately affect 'suitability of D/I price paid' and thus, 'quality of D/I work'. An increase in 'site-specific accuracy of bidding document technical specifications', for example, will result in an increase in the 'accuracy of implementing agency's BoQ', and thus an increase in the 'evaluation team's awareness of price required for high-quality D/I', and so on. Furthermore, an increase in this factor will also increase 'if lump sum payment: suitability of BoQs prepared by bidding DCs', and thus the 'suitability of D/I quotes' and so on. A decrease in the 'site-specific accuracy of bidding document technical specifications', however, will adversely affect the aforementioned factors, and subsequently 'suitability of D/I price paid', and thus, 'quality of D/I work'.

As shown in Figure 3.8, the 'suitability of payment terms in D/I contract', depends on a single factor: 'project manager knowledge of the price and payment terms needed for high-quality D/I work and ability to ensure these are allowed for'. This factor is explained in greater detail in the following sub-system.

Implementing agency protocols sub-system. The focus of the implementing agency protocols sub-system (Figure 3.9) is the factor: 'project manager knowledge of price and payment terms needed for high-quality D/I work and ability to ensure these are allowed for'. This factor reinforces 'suitability of D/I price paid' and thus, 'quality of D/I work', via the procurement process and contract management sub-system (Figure 3.9).

For the factor 'project manager knowledge of price and payment terms needed for high-quality D/I work and ability to ensure these are allowed for', the CLD highlights an important nuance that must be accounted for. For this factor to increase and reinforce the 'suitability of D/I price paid' and thus, 'quality of D/I work', the project manager must be both *knowledgeable* of the price and payment terms and they must be *able* to allow for these. The latter aspect, project manager ability, is a crucial aspect of this sub-system, and thus, the system as a whole – those who have any form of control over the project manager's decisions must allow the project manager to allow for the price and payment terms needed for high-quality D/I work. If they do not, the project manager will not be able to allow for a suitable price and/or suitable payment terms, regardless of their personal knowledge.

As shown in Figure 3.9, project manager ability depends on the 'knowledge among project manager superiors of the price and payment terms needed for high-quality D/I work and their willingness to allow the project manager to allow for these'. If the project manager's superiors are unaware of the price and/or payment terms needed, or if they are aware yet they are unwilling to allow the project manager to allow for these, the project manager will not be able to allow for these in the given project cycle. Multiple issues could lead to an unwillingness among the project manager's superiors. Figure 3.9 highlights one of these, namely, 'extent to which the project manager superiors priori-tize installing high-quality handpumps over meeting number of new water source targets within a given budget and timeframe'. Here the CLD highlights how external pressures, for example, donor or national targets, may adversely affect the project manager's decisions and thus, the 'suitability of D/I price paid' and subsequently, the 'quality of D/I work'.

When then looking at the knowledge aspect (whether project manager knowledge or project manager superior knowledge), Figure 3.9 indicates that this can increase via 'training opportunities for project manager and the proj-ect manager superiors' as well as via the availability of an accurate engineer's estimate for the given site (the latter only applies to knowledge of the price needed for high-quality work).

An additional and somewhat crucial way that knowledge can increase is then seen at the top of Figure 3.9: knowledge can be gained from review-ing the quality of work conducted in previous project cycles and monitoring handpump functionality over time. This is where balancing loops B1 and B2

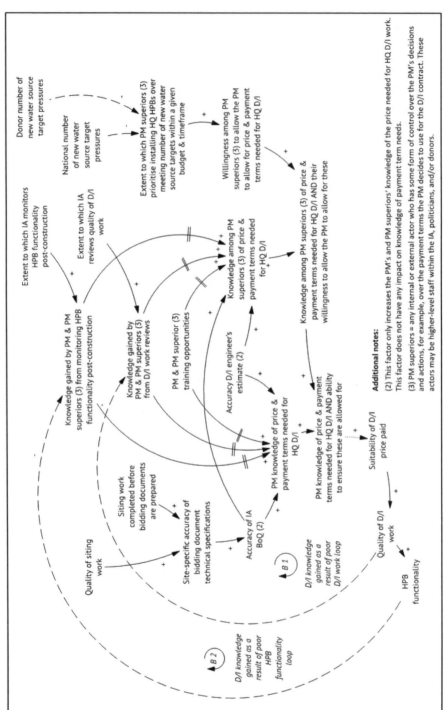

Figure 3.9 Implementing agency protocols sub-system

Solid lines indicate positive arrows, dashed lines indicate negative arrows.

Additional notes:

(2) This factor only increases the PM's and PM superiors' knowledge of the price needed for HQ D/I work. This factor does not have any impact on knowledge of payment term needs.

(3) PM superiors = any internal or external actor who has some form of control over the PM's decisions and actions, for example, over the payment terms the PM decides to use for the D/I contract. These actors may be higher-level staff within the IA, politicians, and/or donors.

come into effect. B1 highlights that as 'quality of D/I work' decreases, knowledge can be gained as to the price and payment terms needed if the same problems are to be prevented in subsequent project cycles. The same is true for loop B2, only in this case it is 'handpump functionality' that drives the balancing loop. It is important to note that both of these loops will only come into effect if 'quality of D/I work' (B1) or 'handpump functionality' (B2) are problematic (if not, there is no need to change the price or payment terms in subsequent project cycles) and if the implementing agency is reviewing the quality of D/I work upon completion (B1) and monitoring handpump functionality post-construction (B2). Without reviews and monitoring, the implementing agency will be unaware of any quality of D/I or handpump functionality problems, hence no new knowledge will be gained from previous mistakes. These loops highlight the importance of implementing agency monitoring and evaluation; without it, there is a risk that the same mistakes will continue from one project cycle to another, with the 'suitability of D/I price paid' and subsequently, the 'quality of D/I work' continuing to suffer over time.

Full D/I price paid CLD. The full D/I price paid CLD (all sub-systems merged) is shown in Figure 3.10. The full CLD highlights the complexity that lies behind the issue of D/I price paid. While legibility is an issue when the CLD is presented in its full form, it does help to show that the issue of price paid for the D/I work is far from simple. A number of factors and actors have the ability to adversely affect the price that is paid for this work, and thus the quality of the D/I work that is then conducted. Please refer to previous sections' sub-systems for a more in-depth (and clearer) view. The ways in which a CLD like this can be used by practitioners is explained in the following CLD utilization section.

CLD utilization: assessing the overall state of the system and identifying intervention points
Having developed and validated a CLD, it is then important to step back and assess the state of the factor of interest and the rest of the system in your own context. For example, this could be within your own handpump drilling projects in the case of this chapter's CLD. If, having reviewed the CLD, you were to note issues within certain factors, it is then important to identify the causal factors that may be leading to these issues along with the intervention points (factors and feedback loops) that, if utilized, will help in relieving the problems within these factors. Without relief, the factor of interest will continue to suffer.

When identifying intervention points (also known as leverage points), it is important to ensure that the 'root' issue is addressed. These will be found in the system's upstream factors. Quick fixes may be possible lower down in the system, yet often these quick fixes will only help improve the state of the factor of interest in the short term. If long-term, sustainable solutions are to be found, the root issues need to be addressed. As explained by Meadows

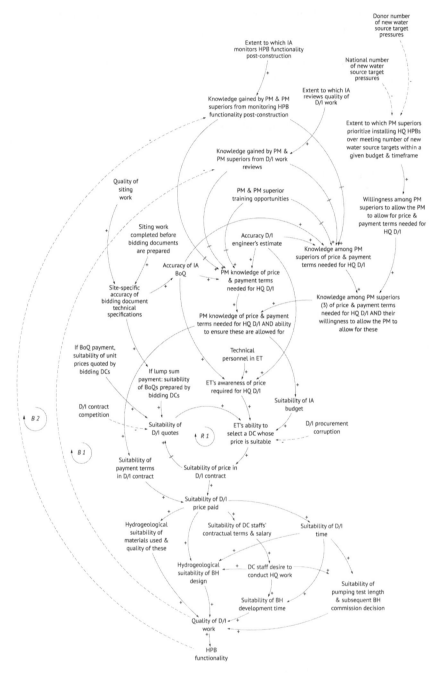

Solid lines indicate positive arrows, dashed lines indicate negative arrows.
See previous sub-system sections for an in-depth explanation of different links.

Figure 3.10 Full suitability of DC price paid and payment terms CLD

(2008), intervention points are points of power. Small changes in these areas can lead to a large shift in the state of the factor of interest. Balancing loops are fundamental when looking for intervention points given their self-correcting nature.

For example, say a given implementing agency was to assess the 'suitability of D/I price paid' for high-quality D/I work within their handpump drilling projects. During this assessment, they notice that the payment terms specified in their DC contracts are causing the 'suitability of D/I price paid' to decrease. The implementing agency would then need to identify:

- why unsuitable payment terms are being specified; and
- the intervention points they could use to increase the suitability of these in future project cycles.

As noted in Figure 3.11, 'suitability of payment terms in D/I contract' depends on: 'project manager knowledge of the price and payment terms needed for high-quality D/I work and ability to ensure these are allowed for'. If, when looking at this factor, the implementing agency notices that unsuitable payment terms are being specified because the project manager is unaware of the payment terms needed for high-quality D/I, the implementing agency would then need to identify intervention points for increasing the project manager's knowledge. As noted in Figure 3.11, project manager knowledge could increase by (dashed ovals in Figure 3.11):

- increasing project manager training opportunities; and
- increasing quality of D/I work reviews upon completion of D/I work and increasing post-construction handpump functionality monitoring.

Through increasing quality of D/I work reviews and handpump functionality monitoring, the balancing loops B1 and B2 will be activated and knowledge will be gained from past mistakes.

Concluding thoughts

It is well known that WASH problems, for example handpump failure, are embedded within complex systems, with a range of factors, actors, dependencies, feedback loops, and time delays all contributing to the given problem. As has been highlighted throughout this chapter, when attempting to solve these problems, there is an essential need to understand and account for the entire system of direct and underlying causal factors known to affect the given problem. When the system structure is not accounted for, our ability to find the most powerful intervention points/solutions is greatly limited (Maani, 2013). Untangling these systems, identifying problematic areas, and thus identifying intervention points for relieving these problematic areas, however, can be a difficult and somewhat confusing task. Thus far, this chapter has provided an overview of a systems thinking tool that can help in this process: CLDs. A step-by-step guide to developing, interpreting, and utilizing a CLD has been

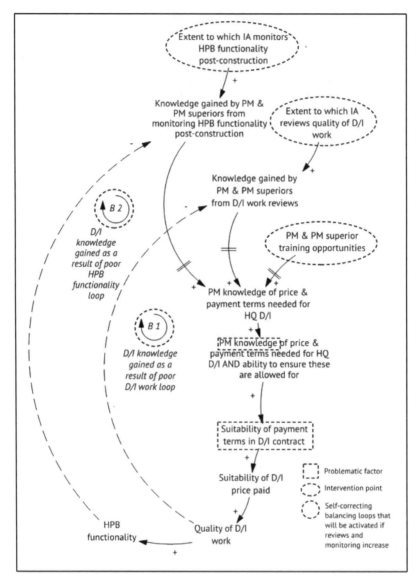

Extract of the D/I price paid CLD, highlighting the intervention points that will help to increase project manager knowledge of the payment terms needed for high-quality D/I, and thus the suitability of the payment terms in D/I contracts.

Solid lines indicate the positive arrows, dashed lines indicate negative arrows.

Figure 3.11 Extract of the D/I price paid CLD

provided, along with an exemplar CLD that focuses on the suitability of the D/I price paid in sub-Saharan Africa handpump drilling projects. In doing so, this chapter has demonstrated how CLDs can help to better develop our understanding of the complexity that lies behind a given problem, and subsequently, how CLDs can help identify the intervention points that should become the focus if a given problem is to be prevented in the future.

In the final section below, we provide a brief case study example, looking at the 'suitability of D/I price paid' in the case of Ugandan handpump drilling projects.

Case study: Ugandan handpump drilling projects

In concluding this chapter, we look at the 'suitability of D/I price paid' in the case of Ugandan handpump drilling projects (collectively across a range of implementing agencies). In doing so, we firstly look at the 'suitability of price in D/I contracts' in Uganda and the state of the causal factors that lie behind this factor, and secondly at the 'suitability of payment terms in D/I contracts' and the state of this factor's causal factors. A series of intervention points are then identified.

The Ugandan information is drawn from 80 semi-structured interviews that were conducted with a range of stakeholders, including staff from the Ministry of Water and Environment (MWE), DC firms, groundwater consultancy firms, the Ugandan Drilling Contractors Association, civil society organizations (CSOs), district water offices (DWOs), and district procurement offices in 2017. Note that in the case of Uganda, CSOs and DWOs are the main implementing agencies for rural water supply. There were 29 implementing agencies interviewed in total (20 DWOs and 9 CSOs).

Price specified in Ugandan D/I contracts

When interviewing DCs in Uganda, it was repeatedly reported that the prices agreed upon in D/I contracts are not suitable for high-quality work. As a result, shortcuts are being taken once on site. D/I contract prices have stagnated over the past decade (approximately UGX20 m (US$5,525 May 2017 exchange rate) per handpump), despite inflation and the devaluation of the Ugandan shilling.

When looking at the causal factors that affect the 'suitability of price in D/I contract', issues were noted in the following D/I price paid CLD factors:

- 'suitability of implementing agency budget';
- 'evaluation team's awareness of price required for high-quality D/I'; and
- 'suitability of D/I quotes'.

All three of these factors were found to be adversely affecting (decreasing) the 'evaluation team's ability to select a DC whose price is suitable', across a number of implementing agencies in Uganda, with this decreasing the 'suitability of price in D/I contracts'. A significant issue was noted within the latter, 'suitability of D/I quotes': DCs are repeatedly under-quoting when bidding for D/I contracts. As alluded to in the procurement process and contract management sub-system explanation section earlier in this chapter, this is an intriguing issue. Why are DCs submitting quotes that are not suitable for high-quality work? The procurement process and contract management sub-system of the D/I price paid CLD (Figure 3.8) shows that four factors could be influencing this issue. Three of these were noted as being problematic in Uganda, as explained below.

- *'D/I contract competition'*. Competition for D/I contracts is high in Uganda, with over 40 DCs operating in-country. As competition has increased, the suitability of the prices quoted has decreased: DCs in Uganda feel that for them to be in with a chance of winning the contract, they must outbid others.
- *'If lump sum payment: suitability of BoQs prepared by bidding DCs'*. If the contract is to be paid as a lump sum, BoQ accuracy at the time of bidding is crucial if the quotes submitted are to be suitable. Without an accurate BoQ, a DC may under-quote, win the contract, and then find themselves without the money required for high-quality work. The blame for inaccurate BoQs, however, cannot necessarily be placed solely on the DCs. Rather, as shown in the procurement process and contract management sub-system of the D/I price paid CLD (Figure 3.8), for accurate BoQs to be prepared, accurate site-specific technical specifications need to be given to the DCs in the bidding documents. This is where the problem lies in Uganda – the bidding document technical specifications are typically inaccurate. Why? The siting work is rarely conducted before the bidding document technical specifications are written (none of the 29 implementing agencies interviewed conducts the siting work before the bidding document technical specifications are written). Instead, bidding document technical specifications are either estimated from past work in the area or they are stock-standard specifications that are used for all the given implementing agency's contracts. DCs in Uganda explained that the inaccuracy of technical specifications limits their ability to submit suitable quotes, with the quality of work then suffering as they try to reduce the overall cost of work, in an attempt to keep within the lump sum price they quoted during bidding.
- *'Suitability of D/I contract price'*. As the suitability of D/I contract prices has decreased in previous project cycles, DCs have begun quoting lower prices in subsequent project cycles, in an attempt to bid within the given implementing agency's known price ranges (reinforcing loop R1, Figure 3.8). DCs in Uganda have established the rough price that different implementing agencies typically pay and are now using these as their benchmark figures when bidding for future work. DCs have realized that if they quote higher than the given implementing agency has paid in the past, they will not win the contract.

D/I contract payment terms in Uganda

Unsuitable D/I contract prices in Uganda are then exacerbated by the payment terms that are being specified in many D/I contracts, with the use of 'lump-sum, no water, no payment' contracts being extremely common (73 per cent of the implementing agencies interviewed use these). Under these contracts, a lump-sum price is agreed upon when the contract is signed. Payment then depends on whether the borehole is deemed successful or unsuccessful upon drilling. If unsuccessful, the DC will not be paid at all.[4] If successful, however, the DC should be paid the full lump-sum price that was agreed upon when the contract was signed, regardless of the final cost of work. It is this full lump-sum payment for successful boreholes that creates a buffer for DCs and helps to cover any recent losses from unsuccessful boreholes or those where the actual cost was greater than the lump-sum price agreed upon in their contract.

While the MWE discourages the use of these lump-sum contracts for a variety of reasons, DCs do not mind these contracts, *when* the payment terms explained above are followed. These payment terms, however, are not always followed, with DCs reporting that many implementing agencies only pay for the work done/materials used (BoQ payment, also known as admeasurement payment in Uganda) for successful boreholes, not the full lump sum. At this point, 'suitability of payment terms D/I contract' greatly decreases, with 'suitability of D/I price paid' along with 'quality of D/I work' then decreasing (Figure 3.10). Interviews with implementing agencies confirmed these unsuitable payment terms: 67 per cent of the DWOs using these lump-sum contracts do not pay the full lump sum for successful boreholes, they simply pay for the work done/materials used. DCs are repeatedly losing their ability to recover the losses from unsuccessful boreholes and any additional costs incurred when the cost of a successful borehole exceeds the lump-sum price. DCs have realized that if they want to stay in business, they will have to cut costs, with aspects such as 'hydrogeological suitability of materials used and quality of these' suffering as a result.

When looking at why these unsuitable payment terms are being used, it was not due to a lack of knowledge among project managers; many of the project managers know that the payment terms they are specifying are unsuitable for high-quality work and that as a result, 'quality of D/I work' has been decreasing. They are unable to change to more suitable payment terms, however, because their superiors will not allow them to ('project manager ability' in Figure 3.10). The same issue was noted when looking at the unsuitable prices implementing agencies are budgeting for the D/I work; unsuitable budgets are not due to a lack of knowledge among project managers – many of the project managers know that the prices they are budgeting are unsuitable for high-quality work. They are not able to increase their budget per handpump, however, as their superiors will not allow them to. Problems within 'knowledge among project manager superiors of price and payment terms needed for high-quality D/I and their willingness to allow the PM to allow for these' must therefore be alleviated within Ugandan implementing agencies.

Intervention points for Uganda

We conclude this chapter by providing an overview of the intervention points that the D/I price paid CLD shows which could be used for relieving some of the issues that were noted within the Ugandan case study. These are outlined in Box 3.1. As highlighted in Box 3.1, there is a major need for D/I price and payment term knowledge to increase among project manager superiors in Uganda, for example, politicians and donors. Alongside this knowledge increase, there must also be an increase in willingness among these superiors to allow their project managers to allow for the necessary prices and payment terms in their budgets and contracts. With such interventions, problems with D/I price paid will slowly be relieved in Uganda, and hence, there will be less of a need for DCs to take shortcuts once on site.

Box 3.1 Summary of the factors that are contributing to unsuitable D/I prices in Uganda and potential intervention points for relieving these issues in the future

Primary problem: Implementing agencies are budgeting unsuitable prices per handpump. Evaluation teams are then being forced to select DCs whose prices are unsuitable for high-quality D/I.

Root issue: Project managers are aware of the price needed for high-quality D/I, but their *superiors will not allow them* to allow for these suitable prices in their D/I budgets.

Possible intervention point(s)
Increase project managers' ability to allow for the price needed for high-quality D/I by:

1. Increasing 'knowledge among project manager superiors of price and payment terms needed for high-quality D/I work'. For this knowledge to increase:

2. 'Accuracy of D/I engineer's estimate' needs to increase. MWE needs to release engineer's estimates that detail the true cost of D/I for a range of drilling depths and borehole designs.

3. 'Accuracy of D/I implementing agency BoQ' needs to increase. Implementing agencies need to ensure that the BoQs they prepare when budgeting the price per handpump are accurate for the given site. To be accurate, the siting work needs to be conducted before the D/I budget is set.

4. 'PM superior training opportunities' needs to increase.

5. 'Extent to which implementing agency monitors handpump functionality post-construction' and 'extent to which implementing agency reviews quality of D/I work' both need to increase. Implementing agencies need to ensure that they are reviewing the quality of D/I work upon completion and monitoring handpump functionality post-construction. Through increasing quality of D/I work reviews and handpump functionality monitoring, the balancing loops B1 and B2 will be activated. These loops will enable knowledge as to the price needed for high-quality D/I work to be gained from previous price mistakes.

Increasing 'willingness among project manager superiors to allow the project manager to allow for the price and payment terms needed for high-quality D/I work'. Increasing superior willingness is crucial if PMs are to be able to allow for suitable prices in their D/I budgets in the future. For willingness to increase:

– PM superiors need to prioritize installing high-quality handpumps, even if this means that the price per handpump needs to increase.

Primary problem: Implementing agency evaluation teams are unaware of the price needed for high-quality D/I work.

Root issue: Firstly, there are no regulated engineer's estimates for D/I work available in Uganda. Secondly, there are accuracy issues with the BoQs that are being prepared by implementing agencies (for use during financial evaluation) because the siting report is not available when these BoQs are prepared.

Possible intervention point(s)

1. Increase 'accuracy of D/I engineer's estimate': MWE needs to release engineer's estimates that detail the true cost of D/I for a range of drilling depths and borehole designs.

2. Increase 'accuracy of implementing agency BoQ': implementing agencies need to ensure that the BoQs they prepare when budgeting the price per handpump are accurate for the given site. To be accurate, the siting work needs to be conducted before the D/I budget is set.

Primary problem: The prices DCs are quoting during bidding are unsuitable for high-quality D/I work.

Root issue: Firstly, there are accuracy issues with the DC bidding document's technical specifications because the siting report is not available when these are prepared. Secondly, DCs have learned the price that implementing agencies are willing to pay (these prices are unsuitable for high-quality D/I work) and are now bidding within these known price ranges.

Possible intervention point(s)

1. The siting work needs to be conducted before the DC bidding documents are prepared, as bidding documents must be site-specific.

2. 'Suitability of price in D/I contract' must increase. Implementing agencies must be known for paying suitable D/I prices (depends on price paid in previous project cycles – R1).

Primary problem: The payment terms implementing agencies are specifying are unsuitable for high-quality D/I work.

Root issue: PMs are aware of the fact that these payment terms are unsuitable; however, *their superiors will not allow them* to change these.

Possible intervention point(s)

Increase project manager ability to allow for the payment terms needed for high-quality D/I by:

1. Increasing 'knowledge among project manager superiors of price and payment terms needed for high-quality D/I work'. For this knowledge to increase:

    –   'PM superior training opportunities' needs to increase.

    –   'Extent to which implementing agency monitors handpump functionality post-construction' and 'extent to which implementing agency reviews quality of D/I work' both need to increase. Implementing agencies need to ensure that they are reviewing the quality of D/I work upon completion, and monitoring handpump functionality post-construction. Through increasing quality of D/I work reviews and handpump functionality monitoring, the balancing loops B1 and B2 will be activated. These loops will enable knowledge as to the payment terms needed for high-quality D/I work to be gained from previous price mistakes.

2. Increasing 'willingness among project manager superiors to allow the project manager to allow for the price and payment terms needed for high-quality D/I work'. Increasing superior willingness is crucial if PMs are to be able to allow for suitable prices in their D/I budgets in the future. For willingness to increase:

    –   PM superiors need to prioritize installing high-quality handpumps, even if this means that the price per handpump needs to increase.

Acknowledgements

This work is part of the Hidden Crisis project within the UPGro research programme – co-funded by the Natural Environment Research Council (UK), the Department for International Development (UK), and the Economic and Social Research Council (UK).

Endnotes

1. NB: the words 'suitable' and 'suitability' are used throughout this chapter and in the CLD that is developed. Any time either of these words is used, they refer to the suitability of [x] for high-quality D/I work. High-quality D/I work is D/I work in which the DC responsible (and its staff) is able to competently and effectively conduct all aspects of this work.

For high-quality D/I work to result, DC staff need to be able to: a) accurately follow the technical specifications given; b) recognize where these technical specifications (for example, the borehole depth) are inappropriate for the hydrogeological conditions found upon drilling; c) accurately decide on the subsequent design change and then implement this; d) use high-quality and hydrogeologically suitable materials and equipment throughout; e) develop the borehole for a suitable amount of time; and f) test pump the borehole for a suitable amount of time and competently decide whether the borehole should be commissioned, and if it is to be commissioned, the pump cylinder depth.

2. Implementing agencies may include, but are not limited to, the central government, local government, non-governmental organizations, community-based organizations, and faith-based organizations.

3. For the purpose of this chapter, we have kept our factor of interest and system boundary rather narrow in order to control the size of the CLD (for practical publishing purposes). If this CLD were to be developed for use in the real-world, aspects such as DC skill-set would need to be included, given the inevitable impact this has on quality of D/I work and subsequent handpump functionality.

4. Does not meet the thresholds specified in the contract for adequate yield and water quality.

References

Adank, M., Kumasi, T.C., Chimbar, T.L., Atengdem, J., Agbemor, B.D., Dickinson, N., and Abbey, E. (2014) 'The state of handpump water services in Ghana: Findings from three districts', in *37th WEDC International Conference, Hanoi, Vietnam.*

Anscombe, J.R. (2011) *Consultancy Services: Quality Assurance of UNICEF Drilling Programmes for BHs in Malawi*, Mangochi, Malawi: Ministry of Agriculture Irrigation and Water Development, Government of the Republic of Malawi.

Bey, V., Magara, P., and Abisa, J. (2014) *Assessment of the Performance of the Service Delivery Model for Point Water Sources in Uganda*, Triple-S Final Research Report, The Hague, Netherlands: IRC.

Bonsor, H.C., Oates, N., Chilton, P.J., Carter, R.C., Casey, V., MacDonald, A.M., Etti, B., Nekesa, J., Musinguzi, F., Okubal, P., Alupo, G., Calow, R., Wilson, P., Tumuntungire, M., and Bennie, M. (2015) 'A hidden crisis: strengthening the evidence base on the current failure of rural groundwater supplies', in 38th WEDC International Conference, Loughborough University, UK.

Engel, S., Iskandarani, M., and del Pilar Useche, M. (2005) *Improved Water Supply in the Ghana Volta Basin: Who Uses it and Who Participates in Community Decision-making?* EPT Discussion Paper 129, Washington, DC: International Food Policy Research Institute, pp. 1–61.

Fisher, M.B., Shields, K.F., Chan, T.U., Christenson, E., Cronk, R.D., Leker, H., Samani, D., Apoya, P., Lutz, A., and Bartram, J. (2015) 'Understanding handpump sustainability: determinants of rural water source functionality in the Greater Afram Plains region of Ghana', *Water Resources Research* 51(10): 1–19 <https://doi.org/10.1002/2014WR016770>.

Foster, T. (2013) 'Predictors of sustainability for community-managed hand-pumps in Sub-Saharan Africa: evidence from Liberia, Sierra Leone, and Uganda', *Environment, Science and Technology* 47(21): 12037–46 <https://doi.org/10.1021/es402086n>.

Gleitsmann, B.A., Kroma, M.M., and Steenhuis, T. (2007) 'Analysis of a rural water supply project in three communities in Mali: participation and sustainability', *Natural Resources Forum* 31(2): 142–50 <https://doi.org/10.1111/j.1477-8947.2007.00144.x>.

Harvey, P.A. (2004) 'Borehole sustainability in rural Africa: an analysis of routine field data', in 30th WEDC International Conference, Vientiane, Laos, 25–29 October 2004 [online], pp. 339–46, <https://dspace.lboro.ac.uk/2134/2109> [accessed 24 August 2018].

Haysom, A. (2006) *A Study of the Factors Affecting Sustainability of Rural Water Supplies in Tanzania*, Dar es Salaam: WaterAid Tanzania.

Hazelton, D.G. (2000) *The Development of Effective Community Water Supply Systems Using Deep and Shallow Well Handpumps*, WRC Report No. TT 132/00, Pretoria, South Africa: WRC.

Hjorth, P. and Bagheri, A. (2006) 'Navigating towards sustainable development: a system dynamics approach'. *Futures* 38(1): 74–92 <http://dx.doi.org/10.1016/j.futures.2005/04.005>.

Hoko, Z. (2008) 'An assessment of quality of water from boreholes in Bindura District, Zimbabwe', *Physics and Chemistry of the Earth* 33(8): 824–8 <http://dx.doi.org/10.1016/j.pce.2008.06.024>.

Hoko, Z. and Hertle, J. (2006) 'An evaluation of the sustainability of a rural water rehabilitation project in Zimbabwe', *Physics and Chemistry of the Earth* 31(15–16): 699–706 <https://doi.org/10.1016/j.pce.2006.08.038>.

Hoko, Z., Demberere, T., and Siwadi, K. (2009) 'An evaluation of the sustainability of a water supply project in Mt Darwin district: Zimbabwe', *Journal of Sustainable Development in Africa* 11(2): 98–112.

Howe, C.W. and Dixon, J.A. (1993) 'Inefficiencies in water project design and operation in the third world: an economic perspective'. *Water Resources Research* 29(7): 1889–94 <https://doi.org/10.1029/92WR02989>.

Katsi, L., Siwadi, J., Guzha, E., Makoni, F.S., and Smits, S. (2007) 'Assessment of factors which affect multiple uses of water sources at household level in rural Zimbabwe: a case study of Marondera, Murehwa and Uzumba Maramba Pfungwe districts', *Physics and Chemistry of the Earth* 32(15–18): 1157–66 <https://doi.org/10.1016/j.pce.2007.07.010>.

Liddle, E. and Fenner, R. (2017) 'Water point failure in sub-Saharan Africa: the value of a systems thinking approach', *Waterlines* 36(2): 140–66 <https://doi.org/10.3362/1756-3488.16-00022>.

Maani, K. (2013) *Decision-making for Climate Change Adaptation: A Systems Thinking Approach*, Gold Coast, Australia: National Climate Change Adaptation Research Facility.

Maani, K.E. and Cavana, R.Y. (2007) *Systems Thinking, System Dynamics: Managing Change and Complexity*, 2nd edn, Auckland: Prentice Hall.

McPherson, H.J. and McGarry, M.G. (1987) 'User participation and implementation strategies in water and sanitation projects', *International Journal of Water Resources Development* 3(1): 23–30 <https://doi.org/10.1080/07900628708722330>.

Meadows, D.H. (2008) *Thinking in Systems: A Primer,* Hartford, VT: Chelsea Green Publishing.

Nyong, A.O. and Kanaroglou, P.S. (2001) 'A survey of household domestic water-use patterns in rural semi-arid Nigeria', *Journal of Arid Environments* 49(2): 387–400 <https://doi.org/10.1006/jare.2000.0736>.

Parry-Jones, S., Reed, R.A., and Skinner, B.H. (2001) *Sustainable Handpump Projects in Africa,* Loughborough, UK: WEDC, Loughborough University.

Sangodoyin, A.Y. (1991) 'Water quality, influence and maintenance of rural boreholes in Nigeria agency', *International Journal of Environmental Studies* 37(1–2): 97–107 <https://doi.org/10.1080/00207239108710620>.

Sara, J. and Katz, T. (1998) *Making Rural Water Supply Sustainable: Report on the Impact of Project Rules,* Washington, DC: UNDP – World Bank Water and Sanitation Program, World Bank.

Sterman, J. (2000) *Business Dynamics: Systems Thinking and Modeling for a Complex World,* Boston, MA: McGraw-Hill.

Walters, J.P. and Javernick-Will, A.N. (2015) 'Long-term functionality of rural water services in developing countries: a system dynamics approach to understanding the dynamic interaction of factors'. *Environment, Science and Technology* 49(8): 5035–43 <http://dx.doi.org/10.1021/es505975h>.

Whaley, L. and Cleaver, F. (2017) 'Can "functionality" save the community management model of rural water supply?', *Water Resources and Rural Development* 9: 56–66 <https://doi.org/10.1016/j.wrr.2017.04.001>.

Wolstenholme, E.F. (2003) 'Towards the definition and use of a core set of archetypal structures in system dynamics', *System Dynamics Review* 19(1): 7–26 <https://doi.org/10.1002/sdr.259 C>.

About the authors

Elisabeth Liddle is a PhD candidate in the Centre for Sustainable Development at Cambridge University. Her Master of Science research at the University of Otago in New Zealand investigated the spatial variability of surface water and groundwater quality in Ndola, Zambia, and the impact of these variations on livelihoods. Having received a Cambridge–Rutherford Memorial Scholarship from the Rutherford Foundation of New Zealand, Elisabeth moved to the United Kingdom in 2015 to pursue her doctoral studies at Cambridge University. Her doctoral research looks at the problem of handpump-borehole failure across sub-Saharan Africa through the lens of systems thinking. Her research is part of the Hidden Crisis project within the UPGro research programme. Elisabeth has published articles in multiple academic journals, including in *Waterlines* and *The Geographical Journal.*

Richard Fenner is Professor of Engineering Sustainability and Course Director for the MPhil in Engineering for Sustainable Development at Cambridge University's Engineering Department. He is a Chartered Civil Engineer and Fellow of the Chartered Institution of Water and Environmental Management. His research interests focus on water, sanitation, and sustainability issues in both developed and developing countries and he has recently worked on projects relating to urban flood resilience in the UK, rural water supply in Africa, and environmental hazards in Bangladesh. He is co-editor of the book *Sustainable Water* (ICE Publishing) and joint author (with Charles Ainger) of *Sustainable Infrastructure: Principles into Practice* (ICE Publishing). Richard has published over 100 journal papers, book chapters, and conference papers and has served on a number of editorial panels for the *Proceedings of the Institution of Civil Engineers*, and also on steering groups for the UK Environment Agency, Construction Industry Research and Information Association (CIRIA), and the Building Research Establishment (BRE). He is the recipient of several awards from the Institute of Civil Engineers including the George Stephenson Gold Medal, the R.A. Carr Prize, and the James Watt Medal, as well as the Senior Moulton Medal from the Institution of Chemical Engineers. He is a Fellow of Wolfson College.

CHAPTER 4
Applying social network analysis to WASH

Duncan McNicholl

Abstract

WASH services are influenced by complex stakeholder interactions that need to be understood and potentially influenced in order to improve service quality and sustainability. Social network analysis provides an opportunity for mapping and rigorously interpreting these stakeholder interactions in order to develop and monitor strategic interventions. Studies using social network analysis can be scaled to fit the scope of any project, and the visual nature of social networks helps to make findings accessible to a wide range of stakeholders.

This chapter presents four approaches to social network analysis in WASH: snowball network analysis; whole network analysis; ego network analysis; and actor and factor analysis. The key to effective application of these methods is defining what questions are being asked and how the information will be used. This chapter outlines considerations for when each method is appropriate with examples from Ghana, Tajikistan, Bolivia, and Uganda in order to help practitioners determine how to best apply social network analysis to their specific areas of interest.

Keywords: social network analysis, stakeholder relationships, institutional development, coordination

Chapter overview

WASH sectors consist of complex interactions involving stakeholders such as governments, communities, private sectors, and NGOs. These relationships influence how WASH services evolve, and where organizations can most strategically contribute to a sector. Interpreting these relationships can be challenging, and Social Network Analysis (SNA) can help practitioners to understand and influence these complex environments. In particular, SNA can be used to identify key stakeholders and gaps in networks in order to make efficient use of existing networks, and to strategically strengthen specific networks to improve WASH service delivery.

The key to using SNA well is first defining what information is needed and how it will be used. This chapter shows how SNA can provide different types

http://dx.doi.org/10.3362/9781780447483.004

of insight into WASH sectors depending on the study design. Each application of SNA requires some important considerations about what data to include and how to capture it. This chapter presents case studies to highlight four different applications of SNA in WASH, and their implications on scope and data collection methods:

- *Snowball Network Analysis*. Used to map networks of stakeholders involved in service delivery that include both known and unknown actors.
- *Whole Network Analysis*. Used to identify gaps, brokers, and communities of coordination in a group of known stakeholders.
- *Ego Network Analysis*. Used to analyse relationships and influences around a specific stakeholder of interest.
- *Actor and Factor Analysis*. SNA combined with qualitative methods is used to analyse how different stakeholder groups relate to different issues.

Social network analysis on its own, however, does not confirm whether network structures are beneficial or detrimental to service delivery. Interpretation by knowledgeable practitioners is still required to critically assess and apply insights from SNA. This chapter will further explore how qualitative data can complement network analysis, and how network analysis might be used as a tool for dialogue among stakeholders to develop strategies for improving WASH service delivery.

An introduction to social network analysis

Social network analysis is used to analyse relationships between actors. It is useful for quantitatively and visually interpreting complex stakeholder interactions, and the methods and analytical approaches can easily be extended to the WASH sector. SNA is particularly applicable because of the need to rigorously yet practically analyse how to strengthen existing interactions, and to consider how new actors or relationships might affect how service delivery systems evolve. The precise methods depend on the question of interest, and practitioners can tailor methods to their needs and budgets.

Choosing the right type of network analysis for the question

The first step in effective use of SNA is defining the network of interest. Findings will depend on these definitions because many different types of stakeholder networks can exist simultaneously. Practitioners should first consider:

- **Who is 'in' the network?** All systems analysis requires the definition of clear scope boundaries. Networks are no exception. A key decision at the outset is to determine if the networks will include a predetermined list of stakeholders, or if new stakeholders will be identified in the course of the study. Networks can even be combinations of issues and stakeholders, as one of the analyses presented in this chapter will show.

- **Which ties are in the network?** Many different tie types can exist between stakeholders. A single relationship might contain information sharing, resource transfers, and power dynamics, among others. These ties can be of different strengths, and can be either one-way or two-way. Practitioners need to consider which types of relationships are of most interest, while also considering how easily data on the relationships can be collected.
- **Which data sources are relevant?** Data can come from either existing records, or can be generated from the study through primary data collection. Emails or meeting attendance records can provide sources of existing data to show where stakeholders communicate with each other or are attending similar events. Surveys, on the other hand, are a means of capturing data that might be difficult or impossible to collect otherwise. Existing data records can be potentially unreliable or unobtainable in the context of rural WASH.

Four case studies will illustrate how the answers to these questions can provide different types of insight into WASH stakeholder networks.

Snowball network analysis

Snowball networks are useful for exploratory network mapping in an unfamiliar stakeholder environment. These are areas where accessing a list of stakeholders is either challenging or the list is likely to miss important stakeholders. Snowball networks can work well in these situations to quickly develop a map of stakeholders and their interactions. Follow-up work can then continue to study the network to rigorously analyse how the network changes over time.

Snowball network analysis was applied to the Ghana WASH sector to analyse how interactions influenced institutional development in district governments (McNicholl, 2017). A complete list of relevant stakeholders was unavailable, and snowball network analysis was therefore appropriate for data collection. The following decisions defined how snowball network analysis was applied in this case study.

Who is in the network?

- A few initial stakeholders were selected as starting points. These were government institutions with a direct mandate in the Ghana rural water sector, and specifically included two district governments of central interest to the study.
- These initial stakeholders were used to identify others from a specific prompt called a 'name generator'. For example, a stakeholder might be asked 'Who are your friends?' as a prompt to generate the names of

Table 4.1 Tie types studied in the Ghana WASH sector snowball network

Tie type	Sub-type (weight)	Description
1. Information	1.1 Download	Information sent from one to the other
	1.2 Discussion	Issues are identified, discussed, and clarified
	1.3 Dialogue	Exploring assumptions together leads to new understanding between stakeholders
2. Resources	2.1 Low	< US$100,000 per year
	2.2 Mid	$100,000–$1 m per year
	2.3 High	> $1 m per year
3. Authority	3.1 Influence	Ability to influence interests of others indirectly
	3.2 Authority	Control; the authority able to enforce consequences for non-compliance
4. Skills	4.1 Consulting	Temporary skill provision to complete a task
	4.2 Training	Providing temporary skill building activities
	4.3 Coaching	Ongoing customized interaction to support participants' ability to overcome challenges
	4.4 Co-development	Supporting another stakeholder to develop their own way of doing things

Source: McNicholl (2017)

other stakeholders. The question used in this study was 'Who do you interact with in the Ghana rural water sector?' The term 'interact' was defined according to the types of ties studied in this network (Table 4.1).

- The network expanded to include newly identified stakeholders according to selection criteria. For example, a researcher might decide to start with five key stakeholders, and expand two degrees of separation from each one. This study applied selection criteria of how many times a stakeholder was identified through the name generator approach to define who to follow up with. Stakeholders had to be mentioned in a minimum of two interviews in order to be included for a follow-up interview.

Which ties are in the network?

- A typology of tie types was derived from a definition of social power (French and Raven, 1959). The terms were adapted to use language familiar to stakeholders in rural WASH sectors, and the ties were weighted to indicate different strengths of interaction. All ties were directional to show the source and target of a tie, and multiple ties could exist in parallel.

Which data sources are relevant?

- Primary interviews were chosen as the data source for the study because detailed information on the tie types was assumed to be difficult to collect from existing records. The interview format also allows participants to express relationships as they are experienced, which might contradict what is formally intended. Interviews were therefore preferred as a method that could capture how the network actually functioned in practice.
- A second decision was to interview a knowledgeable individual to represent each stakeholder. Interviewing all members of a stakeholder, such as a government department, was deemed unfeasible, and individuals with relevant expertise were therefore sought to represent the stakeholder.

Data were collected through a facilitated exercise called egocentric network mapping. Using a piece of flip chart paper, the name of the stakeholder was written in the middle, and other stakeholders identified using the name generator were written on Post-it notes in a circle around the edge of the paper. The different tie types were then explained to the participant, and he or she proceeded to draw arrows representing their relationship. Colours were used to represent tie types, arrows were used to indicate direction, and the number of arrowheads was used to indicate the strength of the tie (Photo 4.1).

Concentric circles can also be used to represent different frequencies of interaction. The Post-it notes representing stakeholders can be placed in these accordingly. The circles can be used to represent weekly, monthly, and yearly frequencies of interaction from innermost to outermost, respectively (Photo 4.2).

Photo 4.1 An egocentric network mapping interview

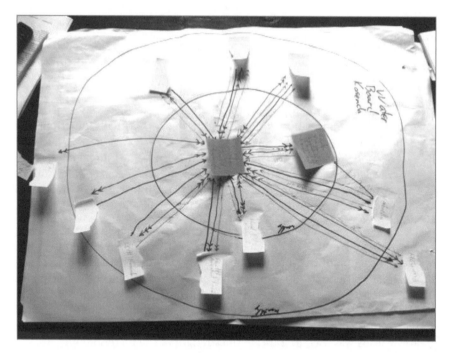

Photo 4.2 An egocentric network including frequencies of interaction in Uganda

Combining all stakeholders and ties from these interviews can then create the snowball network (Figure 4.1). The open-source network software Gephi was used for analysis and visualization of networks throughout this chapter (Bastian et al., 2009).

The resulting snowball network is primarily useful for identifying stakeholders in a sector, visualizing their relationships, and using this initial network to develop further lines of inquiry. Importantly, snowball networks can be useful for identifying gaps that might represent opportunities for strengthening coordination, technical support, and service delivery. Stakeholder names have been omitted from the Ghana snowball network in accordance with the ethical expectations of the study, but including the names can provide a rich basis for considering how specific stakeholders relate to the broader network.

Snowball network analysis does have limitations, however. Firstly, care is needed when selecting the name generator approach to ensure that respondents clearly and consistently provide accurate responses. Even slight differences in phrasing or context can significantly affect responses. Another limitation is that whole network analysis methods cannot be applied to snowball networks. Whole network methods are described in the next section, and they are used to quantify network aspects including the network diameter and which stakeholder is 'most central' to a network. Because of challenges with the name generator approach, there is a risk that any omission might change the number of stakeholders and ties in the network, which can then

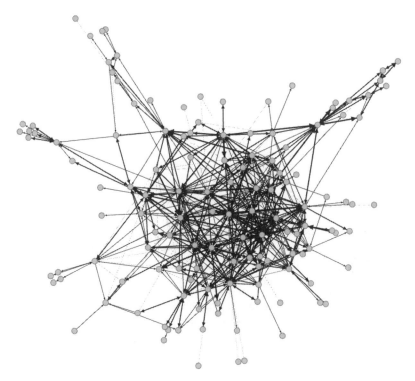

Figure 4.1 The snowball network of WASH stakeholders in Ghana produced from combining network data from individual interviews

affect the overall network structure that is used to calculate diameter and centrality.

Snowball network analysis is therefore a useful starting point that can be used to generate a stakeholder list necessary for whole-network analysis, and for developing questions about specific parts of a network to investigate. Even without quantitative analysis, network visuals can be helpful communication tools. Network visuals can initiate dialogue, or help to effectively and efficiently communicate how sector stakeholders interact.

Snowball networks can also provide a useful basis for more detailed network investigation. The study in Ghana was used as a basis for ego network analysis of two specific local governments by first identifying stakeholders that directly interact with the local governments. Analysis of ego networks is outlined later in this chapter.

Snowball network analysis summary

Good for:

- exploring an unfamiliar network to initially identify relevant stakeholders;
- developing network visualizations for communication purposes; and
- generating hypotheses about the network for further investigation.

Limitations:

- Certain types of quantitative network analysis cannot be performed on snowball networks.
- Name generator questions need to be carefully designed to minimize bias and omissions.

Whole network analysis

Whole networks allow the study of ties between a specific known group of stakeholders. Data collection is designed to capture all network ties between stakeholders without omissions by either accessing existing data records, such as emails or meeting attendance, or by explicitly asking a stakeholder about their interactions with every other stakeholder in the defined network. Ensuring that all network ties are captured provides a stronger basis for quantitative analysis that is not possible with snowball networks. Whole network analysis can be used to answer questions such as:

- How closely connected are stakeholder groups?
- Who is central to the network? Who are gatekeepers?
- Where are stakeholders disconnected from the network?
- How many degrees of separation exist between one side of the network and the other?

These types of analysis cannot be rigorously performed on snowball networks because any missing stakeholders or unidentified ties can change the overall network structure, and therefore the results of whole network analysis.

A study of national WASH stakeholders in Tajikistan illustrates how whole network analysis can be applied in practice. The study has not concluded, but data from a previous snowball network study are used here as an example to illustrate how whole network analysis will be performed when data become available.

Who is in the network?

- A specific group of stakeholders from the Tajikistan Water Supply and Sanitation network.
- The list is available from an existing roster of network membership. The boundaries are therefore clearly defined from the outset.
- Stakeholders not included in the network membership are not included in the study.

Which ties are in the network?

- Information ties were selected as the basis of the study. These are the same information ties defined in the snowball network study applied in Ghana (Table 4.1).

- Snowball network research conducted in Ghana, Malawi, India, Tajikistan, and Bolivia found that 95 per cent of network relationships included an information tie (McNicholl, 2017). Studying undirected information ties was therefore deemed to be the simplest means of identifying where relationships and gaps exist in networks when collecting data on multiple tie types is not feasible.

Which data sources are relevant?

- Primary data collection was considered to be the easiest and most accurate means of data collection in Tajikistan.
- A survey was therefore developed to be filled in at a network meeting whereby participants fill in the strength of their information relationship with others in the network (Figure 4.2).
- The predetermined list makes the development and use of such a survey straightforward.
- The form can then be scanned to quickly input network data for analysis using Formscanner open source software (Borsetta et al., 2017).

Results from the survey can then be combined to produce a whole network for analysis.

Whole networks can be analysed to characterize specific properties of the network (Figure 4.3). The values for the whole network studied in Tajikistan are presented first, followed by a definition of the property and how this property might be interpreted in a WASH stakeholder network context.

Network diameter: 4. Diameter measures the fewest number of ties needed to link the two most distant nodes in a network. In this network it takes four ties to bridge between the most distant stakeholders in the network.

Betweenness centrality: The stakeholder with ID: 1 is the most central. Betweenness centrality measures the likelihood that a node is on the shortest path between any two other nodes in a network. In this case, the stakeholder with ID: 1 is the most likely to be on the path between any two other stakeholders in the network, and is therefore the most central.

Connected components: 1. Counts the number of stakeholder groups that are connected either directly or indirectly. A value of 1 means that a pathway through the network exists that can link a stakeholder to any other. Every stakeholder can be linked to every other stakeholder through ties in this network.

Density: 0.189. A measure of the proportion of ties that exist out of the total number possible among a stakeholder group. A value of 1 would mean that every stakeholder is directly linked to every other in the network. In this case, less than one-fifth of the possible number of ties are observed.

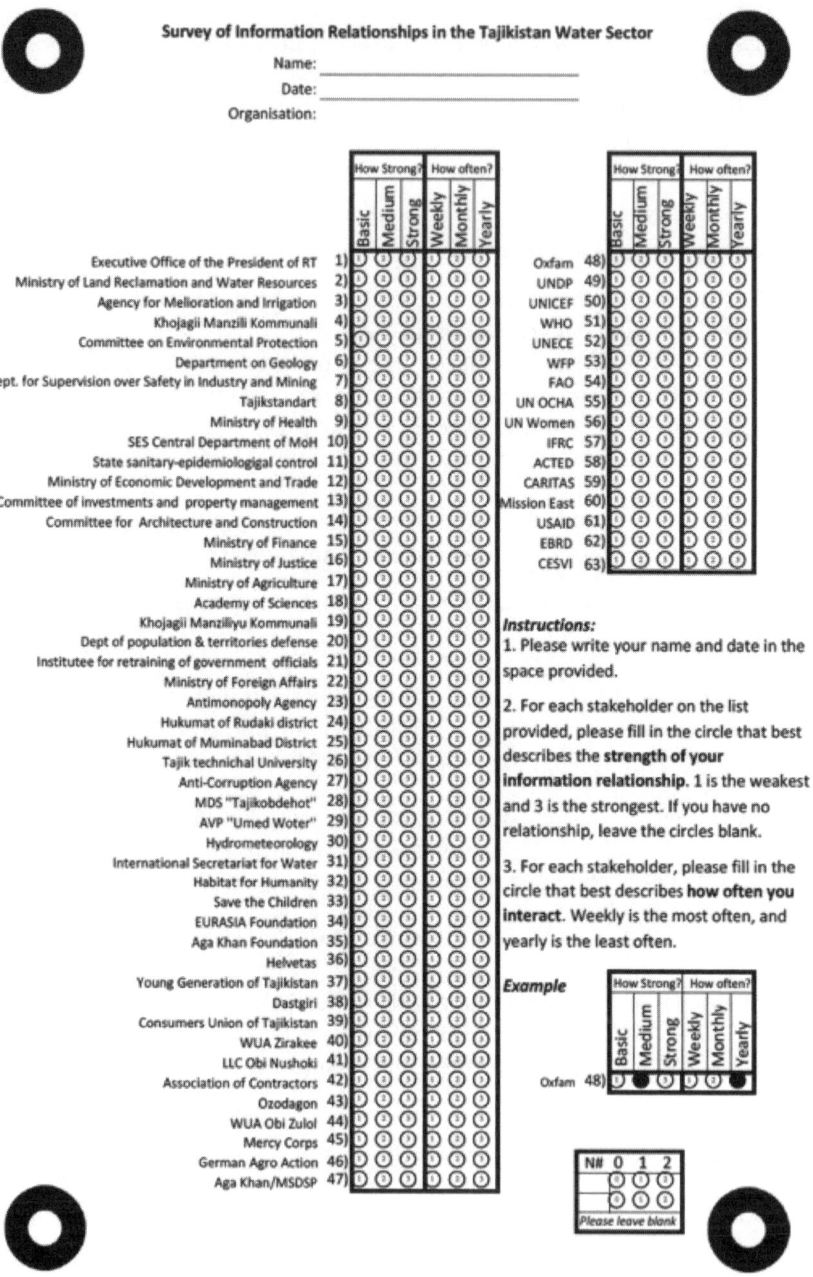

Survey of Information Relationships in the Tajikistan Water Sector

Name: ____________________

Date: ____________________

Organisation:

		How Strong?			How often?		
		Basic	Medium	Strong	Weekly	Monthly	Yearly
Executive Office of the President of RT	1)						
Ministry of Land Reclamation and Water Resources	2)						
Agency for Melioration and Irrigation	3)						
Khojagii Manzili Kommunali	4)						
Committee on Environmental Protection	5)						
Department on Geology	6)						
Dept. for Supervision over Safety in Industry and Mining	7)						
Tajikstandart	8)						
Ministry of Health	9)						
SES Central Department of MoH	10)						
State sanitary-epidemiologigal control	11)						
Ministry of Economic Development and Trade	12)						
Committee of investments and property management	13)						
Committee for Architecture and Construction	14)						
Ministry of Finance	15)						
Ministry of Justice	16)						
Ministry of Agriculture	17)						
Academy of Sciences	18)						
Khojagii Manziliyu Kommunali	19)						
Dept of population & territories defense	20)						
Institutee for retraining of government officials	21)						
Ministry of Foreign Affairs	22)						
Antimonopoly Agency	23)						
Hukumat of Rudaki district	24)						
Hukumat of Muminabad District	25)						
Tajik technichal University	26)						
Anti-Corruption Agency	27)						
MDS "Tajikobdehot"	28)						
AVP "Umed Woter"	29)						
Hydrometeorology	30)						
International Secretariat for Water	31)						
Habitat for Humanity	32)						
Save the Children	33)						
EURASIA Foundation	34)						
Aga Khan Foundation	35)						
Helvetas	36)						
Young Generation of Tajikistan	37)						
Dastgiri	38)						
Consumers Union of Tajikistan	39)						
WUA Zirakee	40)						
LLC Obi Nushoki	41)						
Association of Contractors	42)						
Ozodagon	43)						
WUA Obi Zulol	44)						
Mercy Corps	45)						
German Agro Action	46)						
Aga Khan/MSDSP	47)						

		How Strong?			How often?		
		Basic	Medium	Strong	Weekly	Monthly	Yearly
Oxfam	48)						
UNDP	49)						
UNICEF	50)						
WHO	51)						
UNECE	52)						
WFP	53)						
FAO	54)						
UN OCHA	55)						
UN Women	56)						
IFRC	57)						
ACTED	58)						
CARITAS	59)						
Mission East	60)						
USAID	61)						
EBRD	62)						
CESVI	63)						

Instructions:

1. Please write your name and date in the space provided.

2. For each stakeholder on the list provided, please fill in the circle that best describes the **strength of your information relationship.** 1 is the weakest and 3 is the strongest. If you have no relationship, leave the circles blank.

3. For each stakeholder, please fill in the circle that best describes **how often you interact**. Weekly is the most often, and yearly is the least often.

Example

		How Strong?			How often?		
		Basic	Medium	Strong	Weekly	Monthly	Yearly
Oxfam	48)		●				●

N#	0	1	2

Please leave blank

Figure 4.2 Network survey designed for electronic upload of network data

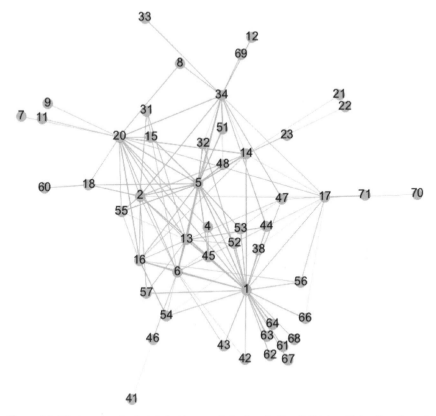

Figure 4.3 Whole network of stakeholders participating in the Tajikistan Water Supply and Sanitation network

Analysis of the whole network shows that a network pathway exists between any two stakeholders, that many stakeholders are directly connected to each other, that even the most distant parts of the network are only a few degrees of separation apart, and that the most central stakeholder in the network is the one with ID: 1.

Whole network properties can be useful for assessing how closely linked network stakeholders are, where network gaps exist, and which stakeholders are most central. Repeating the survey at regular intervals can then be used to monitor changes. Ongoing analysis can consider whether the network becomes more tightly connected, and who the most central stakeholders are over time. Such analysis can quantitatively assess the effectiveness of initiatives designed to strengthen stakeholder networks.

Whole network analysis summary

Good for:

- quantitatively analysing large networks;
- identifying network gaps and the most central stakeholders; and
- rigorously analysing changes in a specific network over time.

Limitations:

- All stakeholders in the network must be identified at the outset; and
- if doing interviews, all stakeholders must be asked about each other stakeholder in the network. A response rate lower than 90 per cent will undermine the validity of quantitative analysis.

Ego network analysis

An ego network considers the stakeholders immediately connected to a stakeholder of interest. Usefully, network analysis can also be applied to smaller pieces of larger networks, including snowball networks. The central stakeholder is called the 'ego', and others with direct ties to the ego are called 'alters' (Figure 4.4).

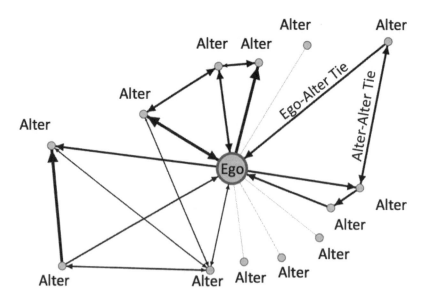

Figure 4.4 Ego network with defined terms
Source: McNicholl et al. (2017)

Ego network analysis can be an easy way to analyse specific points of interest because it usually involves fewer stakeholders than snowball or whole networks. The snowball methods outlined earlier in this chapter were used to generate network data for ego network analysis in several countries, including Bolivia. Interviews began with the egos of interest – three municipal governments. Other stakeholders identified during these initial interviews were interviewed subsequently to identify both ego-alter ties and alter-alter ties. The ego networks of three municipal governments were studied to identify characteristics supporting the development of these institutions for WASH service delivery (McNicholl et al., 2017).

Who is in the network?

- Ego networks include the central stakeholder of interest, and the stakeholders that the ego is directly connected to.
- The alters in an ego network can be determined either in advance or can be identified by the ego.
- In the Bolivian case study, the four municipal governments were the egos, and data from snowball networks were used to identify the stakeholders that the municipalities were directly connected to. This therefore also used a name generator approach.

Which ties are in the network?

- The same typology of ties from the snowball network in Ghana applied to the Bolivian municipalities: information, skills, resources, and authority.
- These four tie types and their sub-categories were found to be an effective classification of network ties. The typology has now been applied in similar studies in Ghana, Malawi, India, Tajikistan, Bangladesh, Bolivia, and Uganda.

Which data sources are relevant?

- Stakeholder interviews, as shown in Photo 4.3, were the data source used. The methods were identical to those used in the Ghana case study mentioned earlier in this chapter.
- The ego network mapping exercise described earlier was used to capture all data in Bolivia.
- Ego stakeholders were interviewed first, and follow-up interviews were conducted with the stakeholders mentioned in these initial interviews.

Data from stakeholder interviews were then combined to produce ego networks for analysis (Figure 4.5).

Ego networks can be analysed by several standard parameters to characterize how the central stakeholder interacts with others. Two quantitative

Photo 4.3 An egocentric network mapping interview in Bolivia

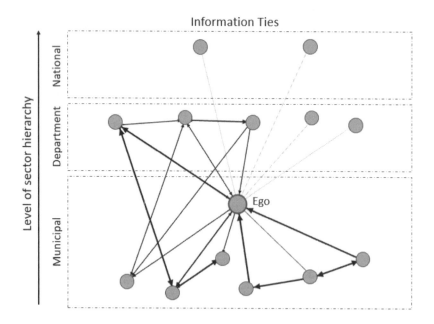

Figure 4.5 Ego network of a case study municipality in Bolivia for information ties

measures are presented in this section, and there are several other measures that can be applied (see Crossley et al., 2015). Standard ego network measures include:

- size – quantifies the number of alters in an ego network;
- homophily – quantifies the proportion of alters that have the same property as the ego out of the total number of alters in the ego network.

Applying measures of size and homophily to the Bolivian municipalities quantifies how many relationships these stakeholders have, and the types of stakeholders they connect to. The study found that the absence of ties to both higher and lower levels of sector hierarchy might limit opportunities for helping these municipalities to improve performance. Findings from ego network analysis can also be useful for identifying stakeholders that are strongly connected to an ego, but only weakly connected to each other. Strategic interventions might then seek to strengthen coordination between specific stakeholders in an ego network.

Ego network analysis summary

Good for:
- analysing interactions around a specific stakeholder of interest. This can be used to identify, for example, opportunities for improving coordination, feedback loops, and access to technical support; and
- quantitatively analysing smaller parts of larger networks.

Limitations:
- Only considers specific parts of a broader network.
- The stakeholder of interest, the ego, may or may not directly affect WASH service delivery.

Additional network measures

Two other network measures can also provide interesting insights into how WASH stakeholder networks behave. As with other network properties, these measures can also be taken at different points in time to quantify how stakeholder networks are changing.

Reciprocity

Reciprocity is a measure of the proportion of network ties that are two-way versus one-way. Quantifying reciprocity for information ties, for example, can potentially quantify the prevalence of feedback loops in a network. A more collaborative network might be expected to show a higher percentage of two-way ties. Reciprocity is calculated by dividing the number of two-way ties by the number of relationships in a network.

Multiplexity

Multiple ties can exist in parallel in stakeholder relationships, depending on the tie types considered. Multiplexity explores the frequency of different tie combinations to understand the likelihood of different tie types in parallel. Resource ties, for example, might almost always be accompanied by strong authority ties, and such analysis might provide useful insights into how stakeholder networks function in practice. Multiplexity analysis can be conducted by quantifying how many times different tie combinations are observed in a network.

Improving social network analysis with qualitative methods

A fundamental limitation of applying SNA to WASH sectors on its own is interpreting the significance of network properties. The structure or quantitative properties of networks are not inherently good or bad. A large number of network ties might have a positive, negative, or neutral effect on WASH service delivery. Qualitative methods can therefore play an important role to complement SNA, helping us to understand whether the observed networks are performing their intended functions, and how the network might be improved.

The network studies described in the snowball and ego network case studies therefore also included a qualitative interview component. Following network mapping exercises, participants were asked to describe aspects of the network that were supporting the management of rural water service delivery to improve. The results were then coded and collated to identify where multiple stakeholders independently identified similar network characteristics as significant. Qualitative description of how networks function in practice was therefore able to inform what to look for in network data to identify network characteristics that support institutional development for WASH service delivery.

Actor and factor networks

Qualitative issues and stakeholder networks can also be combined into a single network for visualization and analysis. A recent study in Uganda funded by United States Agency for International Development (USAID) under the Sustainable WASH Systems Learning Partnership, in collaboration with Aguaconsult and IRC (International Water and Sanitation Centre), illustrates how qualitative and network methods can be combined to produce strategically relevant insights (McNicholl, forthcoming).

A study of Kabarole District in Western Uganda conducted in September 2017 was designed in order to inform strategic interventions to improve WASH service delivery. A whole network analysis was chosen as the appropriate scoping because all relevant stakeholders were able to be identified prior to data collection. The study continued with the use of the tie types defined earlier in this chapter (Table 4.1): information, skills, resources, and authority. Each stakeholder in the network was interviewed individually to identify their interactions, and the resulting data were combined to produce a whole network for analysis.

Whole network analysis was first used to identify the most central stakeholders. Analysis identified that political leaders at both district and more local levels were central to the network because of their relationships that bridge multiple levels of hierarchy. Identifying the most central stakeholders provides a possible intervention point for practitioners to, for example, improve coordination or disseminate information.

Network analysis can help to identify who to engage, but qualitative analysis is needed to identify which issues to tackle. In addition to the network analysis, qualitative interviews with participating stakeholders were transcribed and coded to identify perceived successes, challenges, and potential solutions for improving WASH service delivery in Kabarole.

Identified themes can be directly incorporated into networks for analysis. Network and qualitative data can be combined to show which stakeholders identified which issues, and how these stakeholders relate to each other. Two issues can be considered to illustrate how different stakeholder groups perceive issues. The first issue is coordination. Coordination was viewed as a positive dynamic among a closely related group of stakeholders (Figure 4.6). Stakeholders at local levels of the sector hierarchy, however, perceived institutional leaders to be neglecting their duties towards WASH, and these local stakeholders are not all directly connected to each other (Figure 4.7). Network

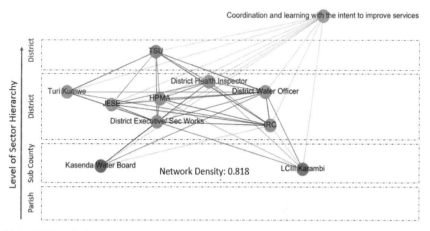

List of Abbreviations

HPMA   Hand Pump Mechanic's Association
IRC   International Water and Sanitation Centre
JESE   Joint Effort to Save the Environment
LCIII   Local Council 3 Chairman
TSU   Technical Support Unit

Figure 4.6 Stakeholders that identified coordination as a positive factor and their relationships
Source: McNicholl (forthcoming)

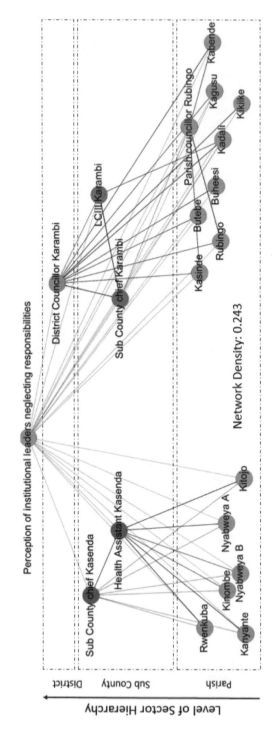

Figure 4.7 Stakeholders that perceived institutional leaders to be neglecting their responsibilities and their relationships
Source: McNicholl (forthcoming)

density provides a measure of how closely connected these stakeholders are. A value of 1 means that every stakeholder is connected to every other one in the network.

Identifying these issues and who they are perceived by then provides further insight for developing intervention strategies. Identifying these issues, who described them, and how these stakeholders relate to each other can provide the basis for potentially forming coalitions to tackle commonly perceived challenges. These results will be now be used by stakeholders in Kabarole to collaboratively address WASH service delivery challenges, and the actor and factor network analysis provides a useful starting point for prioritizing where to work.

Summary

Social network analysis has the potential to improve strategic engagement of WASH stakeholder networks in several ways. Identifying the most appropriate methods will depend on the context, available resources, and intended use of findings.

At its most basic application, network studies can be used to identify network stakeholders and their relationships. This analysis can provide the basis for critical reflection on how WASH stakeholder networks function, and be used to develop questions for further investigation.

SNA can further be used to analyse a known network in order to identify intervention points. Identifying central stakeholders can inform where leverage points might exist in a network. Whole network analysis can also be used to monitor network properties over time to identify changes in relationships.

Ego network analysis can be used to study interactions around a particular stakeholder of interest. Such studies might require fewer resources than whole network studies, and can be applied in specific intervention areas to inform strategies.

SNA can be considerably improved by incorporating qualitative methods to judge the quality of stakeholder interactions. As shown with the actor and factor networks studied in Uganda, combining qualitative methods with network analysis can further inform opportunities for intervention by identifying how specific stakeholders relate to issues and to each other.

All of these methods can be used to develop strategies, improve relationship management, and to monitor change with quantitative rigour. SNA need not be overly expensive or time consuming in order to be useful – it just needs clear intent and selection of proper methods for the question at hand. WASH sectors will continue to be complex environments involving many issues and stakeholders, and SNA provides effective tools for assessing strategic options and for monitoring change.

References

Bastian, M., Heymann, S., and Jacomy, M. (2009) *Gephi: an open source software for exploring and manipulating networks*, in International AAAI Conference on Weblogs and Social Media.

Borsetta, A., Young, C., Lo, G., and Young, K. (2017) Formscanner <www.formscanner.org/> [accessed 3 April 2017].

Crossley, N., Bellotti, E., and Edwards, G. (2015) *Social Network Analysis for Ego-Nets*, SAGE Publications Ltd.

French, J.R.P. Jr, and Raven, B. (1959) 'The bases of social power', in D. Cartwright (Ed.), *Studies in Social Power*, pp. 150–67, Ann Arbor, MI: University of Michigan.

McNicholl, D. (forthcoming) *Actors and Factors Affecting WASH Service Sustainability in Kabarole District, Uganda*, Washington, DC: United States Agency for International Development.

McNicholl, D. (2017) *Characteristics of Stakeholder Networks Supporting Institutional Development in Rural Water Service Delivery*, Cambridge, UK: University of Cambridge.

McNicholl, D., McRobie, A., and Cruickshank, H. (2017) 'Characteristics of stakeholder networks supporting local government performance improvements in rural water supply: cases from Ghana, Malawi, and Bolivia', *Water Alternatives* 10(2): 134–54.

About the author

Dr Duncan McNicholl has nearly 10 years of experience in the WASH sector in Africa, Asia, and South America. He was formerly the Program Manager of the Water and Sanitation Team of Engineers Without Borders Canada in Malawi, and is currently the General Manager of Whave Solutions Ltd, a Ugandan non-profit social enterprise that provides preventive maintenance services for community water sources that serve over 140,000 people. Duncan holds a PhD in Engineering from Cambridge University, where he studied how stakeholder networks influence institutional development for managing rural water supply, and he continues to research how service delivery systems evolve to reliably provide WASH access globally. He rather likes giraffes.

CHAPTER 5

Social-ecological system resilience for WASH

Jeremy Kohlitz, Naomi Carrard, and Tim Foster

Abstract

In a rapidly changing world, WASH services are often exposed to a range of unpredictable social, environmental, economic, and physical disturbances that disrupt WASH access. Social-ecological system (SES) resilience thinking can inform WASH service delivery approaches that adapt to changing conditions in order to sustain access for users rather than resist change. In this chapter, we familiarize readers with SES resilience thinking and consider its application to WASH services. We outline three key processes that practitioners can follow to get themselves and other stakeholders into an SES resilience mindset: mapping WASH systems, considering SES resilience principles, and identifying areas for interventions. We provide illustrative examples and resources to assist practitioners in thinking about how SES resilience concepts can be used to plan for WASH services that are flexible and adaptive. We also consider some limitations and pitfalls to SES resilience concepts to encourage readers to take a critical approach.

Keywords: disturbances, resilience, social-ecological, uncertainty, WASH

OVER THE PAST TWO DECADES, the world has made substantial progress on expanding the coverage of access to basic water and sanitation services. While there is still much work to be done to achieve universal access, the Sustainable Development Goals (SDGs) compel us to also consider the quality and sustainability of water and sanitation services. Such a focus is sorely needed given freshwater over-extraction, climate change, high rates of hardware failure, environmental pollution, and other disturbances that increasingly threaten to disrupt the delivery of adequate WASH services (Moriarty et al., 2013; Hutton and Chase, 2016; Carrard and Willetts, 2017) and reverse hard-won gains.

Systems thinking offers pathways for planning, designing, and sustaining WASH services that go beyond conventional technocratic approaches. The WASH sector has long recognized that simply designing WASH infrastructure to be more physically robust is insufficient for sustaining WASH services. Rather, systems thinking directs us to consider the role of the network of relationships between various WASH actors, water resources, ecosystems, and

http://dx.doi.org/10.3362/9781780447483.005

technologies in enabling sustainable services. Social-ecological system (SES) resilience is a strand of systems thinking that can stimulate us to think differently about WASH in order to develop services that absorb disturbances while maintaining their functionality.

The SES resilience approach views WASH services as continuously changing systems that are composed of interacting social and ecological/environmental parts (hence the term social-ecological system). Decades of experience in the field of natural resources management, with contributions coming from a variety of social and environmental sectors, has culminated in resilience principles for SESs that can be usefully applied to WASH. These principles promote flexibility and adaptiveness instead of resistance to change. Understanding WASH as SESs and putting resilience principles into practice offers valuable insights on developing WASH services that are sustainable over the long term.

In this chapter, we begin by describing the SES resilience approach and its purpose. We then outline the three main processes of the approach: mapping WASH, considering principles of SES resilience, and identifying areas for intervention. Finally, we discuss some limitations and pitfalls of the SES resilience approach and conclude with our overall thoughts on resilient WASH.

The SES resilience approach

Fundamentally, we define resilient WASH services as WASH with the capacity to absorb disturbances and reorganize in order to continue providing the desired level of service. Disturbances are events that happen suddenly and intensely (shocks) or gradually and chronically (stresses) that interrupt the quality, availability, continuity, affordability, physical accessibility, or acceptability of adequate WASH services. Disturbances can be environmental (e.g. a storm), technical (e.g. a hardware failure), social (e.g. a dispute), or economic (e.g. a market fluctuation). Sometimes disturbances are expected. More often, they come as a surprise. Disturbances are *absorbed*, meaning that changes in WASH caused by the disturbances are tolerated (i.e. not necessarily resisted) as long as the components of the system (the WASH actors, technologies, and environmental resources considered to be a part of the system) can reorganize to ensure that WASH access is sustained. *Reorganize* here means that one or more of the WASH components adjusts to a disturbance or change in conditions. For example, people within a rural community may switch between different water sources to meet different water needs depending on seasonal disturbances (Elliott et al., 2017).

The purpose of the SES resilience approach for WASH is to develop flexibility and a capacity to work under uncertainty such that a WASH service is able to change and adapt to disturbances as needed to sustain access for its users. This contrasts with conventional 'command and control' approaches that aim to predict specific disturbances and design WASH services to resist them; for example, climate-proofing a latrine to make it more physically robust in the face of a projected increase in flooding events due to climate change.

Resilience can be strengthened through accounting for the key systems that comprise a WASH service and the interactions between them, and through the practice of resilience principles.

In this section, we outline three key processes to applying an SES resilience lens to WASH: mapping WASH, considering principles of SES resilience, and identifying areas for interventions. We provide examples of how these processes might be applied in practice throughout. Following these processes not only helps to design actions to build resilience, but is also resilience-building itself when service providers are included because the processes help to develop a complex systems thinking mindset.

Mapping WASH

Mapping the systems that make up a WASH service and developing an understanding of how they interact with one another contributes toward building resilience. The purpose of mapping is to determine the most critical components supporting the core functionality of WASH services and find what or whom is influenced by the WASH service. Mapping can be done on systems that already exist or prospectively on a planned WASH service. Mapping helps to characterize the relationships between WASH service systems and give WASH managers an idea of where resilience can be built into the service.

There are a number of existing tools and approaches that may assist a mapping exercise. For urban sanitation, for example, shit flow diagrams provide a structured methodology (including online tools) to understand the flow of excreta throughout the sanitation service chain (see Neely (2019) for a resource). Emerging work also seeks to track the flow of pathogens through an urban environment in order to guide service delivery efforts to address the greatest impacts to public and environmental health (Mitchell et al. 2016; Mills et al. 2018). Causal-loop diagrams, diagrams that visually map out system variables and their relationships using simple symbols and labels, can be an effective way of characterizing interactions between important system components. (For basic guidance on creating a causal-loop diagram, see Neely (2019)). The application of causal-loop diagrams to rural water supplies is demonstrated by Liddle and Fenner (2019) and by Neely and Walters (2016). For social considerations, Social Network Analysis can be used to map relationships between various actors (see McNicholl, 2019). Political economy analysis approaches can also assist with mapping the key actors involved across community, government, private, and development aid sectors, bringing to light the incentives and power structures that shape how decisions about services are made (Manghee and Poole, 2012; ODI, 2012).

Whichever approach is used, social systems (e.g. communities, service providers, government authorities, etc.), environmental systems (e.g. water resources, soils, aquatic ecosystems, etc.), and technological systems (e.g. WASH infrastructure) should be considered. The mapping exercise should also be done collaboratively with multiple stakeholders so that a shared understanding of the key components of WASH can be developed. It is not possible, or desirable, to exhaustively map every component of the system. Rather, system mapping is meant to explore and build consensus about what is important to consider.

Considering principles of social-ecological system resilience

Research on the factors that build SES resilience is still emerging, but resilience experts have begun to reach some consensus. Management of the principles listed in Table 5.1 within an SES is believed to build resilience by enhancing the ability of the SES to absorb disturbances and reorganize. For a deeper discussion on the principles and their meaning, we refer readers to Biggs et al. (2012, 2015).

An assessment of whether these principles are being reflected in a given WASH service, or how they can be implemented in a prospective service, can give stakeholders insight on the level of resilience of the service. An example of resilience in a rural water service is discussed in Box 5.1. Resources that describe activities for assessing SES resilience, and operationalizing the SES resilience principles, are listed in Neely (2019).

Table 5.1 SES resilience principles

Principle	Definition
Maintain diversity and redundancy	Optimize levels of diversity and redundancy of SES components so that there are multiple options and insurance for responding to disturbances
Manage connectivity	Understand the way and degree to which SES components are connected to one another, and strengthen connections that spread useful material or information while weakening connections that propagate disturbances
Broaden participation	Actively engage stakeholders in management and governance processes
Promote polycentric governance systems	Implement multi-scalar, nested, and collaborative governance systems that are matched to the scale of the problem
Encourage learning and innovation	Encourage learning through experimentation and monitoring. Promote adaptive management and adaptive governance
Foster complex adaptive systems thinking	Promote a worldview or mental model that views the world as comprising dynamic and interacting systems

Source: Adapted from Biggs et al. (2015)

Box 5.1 Resilience snapshot: a rural water service in Vanuatu

Uripiv is a small island, 1 km² in size, located in a rural area of the Malampa province of Vanuatu. A community of about 700 people lives on Uripiv and manages its own water services which include hand-dug wells and domestic rainwater harvesting systems. The water service system here reflects SES resilience principles in a couple of ways. During dry spells, the rainwater storage tanks run dry, but water needs can still be met by the wells. Conversely, during heavy rainfall, the wells are contaminated by surface runoff, but rainwater tanks fill up. Multiple water resources in this setting thus bestow flexibility (Diversity principle). The community is also closely connected to the National Disaster Management Office (NDMO) through a community member that was networked with NDMO authorities. NDMO authorities at the national level detect climatic disturbances and communicate them to the community through their network, thus giving households time to prepare their water supplies for the incoming disturbance (e.g. cyclone or drought) (Connectivity and Polycentricity principles).

In other ways, SES resilience is being compromised. The growing community is increasingly clearing vegetation for new homes and plantations. Unwittingly, these activities are compacting the topsoil and degrading ecosystems that regulate surface runoff, thus resulting in more frequent flooding and contamination of the wells. Some community members are also seeking to install pumps at the wells which risks salinization because the shallow groundwater lens sits just above seawater. Raising awareness of the community on the interactions between their water services and the natural environment could help them manage these issues (Foster systems thinking principle).

Every situation is unique, so how the principles can be put into practice will differ between sites. Viewing WASH as an SES and assessing the resilience principles are not meant to provide an objective measure of WASH resilience. Instead, these exercises build knowledge on the critical components of WASH, how they interact with one another, and how these interactions influence resilience through influencing the capacity to absorb disturbances and reorganize. Armed with this knowledge, practitioners can begin to design interventions to further strengthen WASH resilience.

Identifying areas for intervention

Mapping WASH service systems and assessing the degree to which resilience principles are reflected in the service sets the stage for designing interventions to build resilience. WASH services, especially those at bigger scales such as cities, can be highly complex. The mapping exercise helps to identify which components of WASH are most critical for sustaining core functions of different stages of service delivery (e.g. containment, removal, transport, and disposal/reuse for sanitation, and abstraction, treatment, delivery, and collection for water). Based on the prior knowledge of participants, the mapping exercise can also identify system components that are close to failure and sensitize participants as to how the effects of a possible failure could ripple through the systems. The most critical and fragile components of the WASH service systems should be prioritized for resilience interventions.

The resilience principles provide guidance on different ways in which resilience can be built. Some principles pertain to the management and governance of WASH (e.g. Learning and innovation) while others can be applied to WASH infrastructure, social systems, and the environmental systems on which WASH services depend. Based on which components of the WASH service need strengthening and the local context, it may make sense to focus on one principle over the others.

Table 5.2 demonstrates possible examples of what the principles look like when they are practised in a WASH context. These examples are not intended to be a prescriptive list of 'to-do' actions in any situation, but rather assistance for understanding the resilience principles.

Applying an SES resilience lens to service delivery does not require a separate process, but can be integrated with existing planning initiatives. In the urban sanitation sector, for example, there are opportunities to consider the relevance of resilience principles when going through a planning process or considering pathways for achieving the SDG6 target of safely managed sanitation services for all. There is strong alignment between resilience principles and emerging thinking on best practice urban sanitation, with programmes such as Citywide Inclusive Sanitation emphasizing the need to address complexity, consider diverse solutions, prioritize inclusion, and ensure integration (CWIS, 2016). Applying a resilience lens within city sanitation planning processes may assist in identifying practical strategies for realizing these ideals. However, at times, resilience planning can come into tension with more conventional development planning as Box 5.2 illustrates (page 87).

Limitations and pitfalls

The SES resilience approach is useful for supporting WASH services that are flexible and environmentally sustainable, but practitioners must be aware of its limitations and pitfalls, which can create adverse effects. We highlight five such drawbacks in this section: the cost of resilience, unequal distribution of resilience, the disruptive potential of power and politics, data availability, and the desirability of resilience.

First, building resilience can be costly and often comes at the expense of efficiency. Building diversity and redundancy through the installation and maintenance of multiple types of WASH facilities requires more financial resources than providing only a single option.

Table 5.2 Examples of SES resilience principles applied to WASH

Principle	Possible applications to WASH	How does it build resilience?	Example
Diversity and redundancy	Communities have access to different types of water supplies and sanitation facilities	It is less likely that a single type of disturbance cuts off all WASH access	Intense rainfall may contaminate wells but users can access water from rainwater harvesting systems if they are also available
	Spare parts for water supplies and sanitation facilities are readily available	Broken technological components can be replaced to quickly restore degraded levels of service	Hand pump spare parts are readily available to restore water continuity
	Multiple people have knowledge of how to operate and repair WASH technologies	Knowledge on sustaining services is not lost if an individual person departs	Multiple people in a community are trained in WASH operation and maintenance
	Water resource and catchment habitats are home to high levels of plant and animal biodiversity	Biodiversity strengthens the capacity of the natural environment to purify, regulate, and store freshwater	Healthy aquatic ecosystems have some capacity to treat wastewater through processes such as denitrification, adsorption, and filtration
Connectivity	WASH infrastructure is decentralized/modular	Failures are isolated such that they do not spread to other users	Failures of on-site sanitation facilities (e.g. septic tanks) are contained locally and do not cause widespread service issues
	WASH users, managers, and service providers are closely connected to external support agencies	Support agencies can provide resources to maintain services when a disturbance is experienced	Utility service providers are members of associations that share advice on managing climate change risks
	Water resources are not cut off from adjacent ecosystems	Adjacent ecosystems can mitigate disturbances or facilitate ecosystem service recovery following a disturbance	Vegetation on land helps attenuate pollutants in surface runoff that enter streams during intense rainfall

(continues)

Table 5.2 (*continued*)

Principle	Possible applications to WASH	How does it build resilience?	Example
Participation	All WASH stakeholder groups are listened to and considered in decision-making on the planning, implementation, management, and evaluation of WASH services	Wider knowledge bases can be drawn on to detect, interpret, and respond to disturbances to WASH services	Women identify safe areas for building WASH facilities so that women are unafraid to access the facilities
Polycentricity	Local level issues with WASH are dealt with by local service providers and authorities. Broader scale issues are dealt with by authorities at the scale of the issue	Local actors can react more quickly to disturbances and have place-specific knowledge. Broader scale authorities can respond to disturbances that are beyond the reach of local actors	Cities manage local pollution threats to a river system and coordinate with regional, national, or international authorities that manage riverine issues that cross borders
Learning and innovation	WASH managers and service providers monitor and evaluate service levels, and learn how certain disturbances affect them	Managers and service providers can detect and react more quickly to degradation of service and adjust service delivery so that it is less sensitive to disturbances	Water quality is routinely monitored, corrective action is immediately taken when quality is compromised, and control measures are put in place to prevent recurrence of the issue (e.g. climate resilient Water Safety Plans (WHO, 2017))
	WASH NGOs continually trial new technologies, service management schemes, and environmental resource management schemes	WASH technologies and management schemes adapt to the changing world around them	New mobile phone services are used to monitor WASH service levels and report issues to service providers
Foster complex adaptive systems thinking	WASH stakeholders learn to think of WASH services as complex adaptive systems through lessons and case studies from this book and elsewhere	A holistic view of the systems that contribute to WASH service delivery and how they interact makes it less likely that important dimensions are neglected	See case studies throughout this book

---

Box 5.2 Resilience dilemma: hand pumps in Cambodia

Building resilient systems can, at times, involve trade-offs. Strengthening resilience in one area of the system may weaken it in another. For example, the
gamut of rural water supply technologies can present an inverse relationship
between reliability and reparability. An instructive case in point is in rural
Cambodia, where low-lift suction hand pumps can often be seen alongside
more robust piston hand pumps. Some users and implementers opt for the
more expensive piston hand pump because it breaks down less often, and
can lift groundwater from a greater depth, thereby insuring against the risk
of future drawdown. Yet its superior technical performance reduces demand
for spare parts and undermines supply chains. Repairing piston hand pumps
may also require specialist tools and technical know-how. In response to
these drawbacks, the majority of households and implementers opt for a
lower-cost suction hand pump. While it breaks down more often and is more
sensitive to environmental change, it is easier to fix and spare parts are
readily available. This dilemma serves to illustrate that building resilience in
one component of the WASH services can have effects that ripple through to
other components. The mapping exercise can help to plan for some of these
cascading effects.

Decentralization of WASH infrastructure may make it more difficult to achieve
economies of scale in the near term. Innovation does not always succeed and
can be a less efficient means of improving WASH services than 'tried-and-true'
approaches. This is significant in a development context where WASH users
and service providers are frequently limited financially. However, additional
investment is worthwhile in the long term if it enables uninterrupted delivery
of adequate WASH services.

Second, resilience is not always spread equally among WASH users. For
example, a mobile phone service for reporting water point failures to service
providers is an innovation that can help build resilience by increasing connectivity between users and providers, but it may disproportionately benefit
areas with better mobile phone reception. Or, a community may increase
its resilience through the development of multiple types of improved water
points, but the benefits will not be realized for some people if they are unable
to physically access the range of options. Thus, it is important to ask 'who
benefits?' when a particular intervention is being recommended.

Third, the SES resilience approach risks overlooking issues of power and
politics that are impactful on sustaining WASH services. For example, del-
egating responsibilities to local WASH authorities under a polycentric governance approach may fail if the power to make certain decisions and to
control budgets is not also delegated. Also, under a polycentric approach,
local WASH institutions can clash and develop rivalries with one another

if they are not well coordinated and regulated. The SES resilience approach should not be taken apolitically. Practitioners must be mindful of how social and political structures can subvert the resilience principles and reproduce inequalities. The political economy analyses referenced earlier in this chapter can shed light on issues of power and equality so that they can be more readily addressed.

Fourth, major gaps in data availability can make it difficult to map WASH and assess its resilience. Collecting data and monitoring important parameters as promoted by the SES resilience principle on learning and innovation can help to address these gaps.

Finally, it is not necessarily desirable to build more resilient WASH services in any given situation. Some WASH services are, by their nature, inherently environmentally unsustainable or discriminatory against certain social groups. In some cases, stakeholders may aspire for what they perceive to be a better WASH service (e.g. a shift from a community-managed WASH service to a utility-managed one). In these situations, it may not be desirable to build the resilience of the current service. It is important to note that different stakeholders will hold different perceptions about what is desirable. The mapping exercise is an opportune time to engage different perspectives on whether it is desirable to build the resilience of a current WASH service or seek to transform it into something fundamentally different.

Conclusion

WASH resilience is not a standard or static outcome to be attained, but rather an ever-changing process that is unique to each situation. The SES resilience approach views WASH services as complex dynamic systems that function best when managers encourage and leverage their ability to adapt rather than attempt to restrain change and impose rigidness (Box 5.3). This chapter has outlined generic processes and principles that will assist practitioners in harnessing complexity and change to build resilience in WASH. These provide a starting point for the integration of resilience thinking into WASH programming and practice. From here, testing and refining of approaches is needed · to build capacity and evidence about what SES resilience 'looks like' for water and sanitation service systems across rural and urban contexts.

Importantly, the human element must be central to any process. Key stakeholder groups should be engaged at each stage of applying the SES resilience approach to ensure equity and capitalize on the value multiple knowledge holders bring. Before any interventions are identified, inclusion of WASH users in resilience mapping, assessment, and planning will itself build system resilience by fostering learning and recognition of the interconnections that make a WASH service function. The intended result is that WASH will be flexible and adaptive in a rapidly changing world, ensuring continuity of services.

Box 5.3 Practitioner perspective of WASH resilience in El Salvador

From a practitioner perspective, resilience to shocks and disturbances is key to the sustainability of a WASH service. Recently, I visited a water system with 2,000 household connections in El Salvador that is fully functioning after 15 years. It has withstood major disturbances including significant flood damage to the physical infrastructure in 2011, and criminal gang activity that profoundly affected social and economic capital across the service area from 2015 to 2017. Using SES resilience analysis to better understand the reasons why some water services are able to reorganize and continue to grow and expand despite disturbances that cause others to fail, will be an important contribution to achieve sustainable WASH services for all.

Source: Michelle Whalen.

References

Biggs, R., Schlüter, M., Biggs, D., Bohensky, E., BurnSilver, S., Cundill, G., Dakos, V., Daw, T., Evans, L., Kotschy, K., Leitch, A., Meek, C., Quinlan, A., Raudsepp-Hearne, C., Robards, M., Schoon, M., Schultz, L., and West, P. (2012) 'Toward principles for enhancing the resilience of ecosystem services', *Annual Review of Environment and Resources* 37(1): 421–48 <http://dx.doi.org/10.1146/annurev-environ-051211-123836>.

Biggs, R., Schlüter, M., and Schoon, M.L. (eds) (2015) *Principles for Building Resilience: Sustaining Ecosystem Services in Social-Ecological Systems*, Cambridge: Cambridge University Press.

Carrard, N. and Willetts, J. (2017) 'Environmentally sustainable WASH? Current discourse, planetary boundaries and future directions', *Journal of Water Sanitation and Hygiene for Development* 7(2): 209–28 <http://dx.doi.org/10.2166/washdev.2017.130>.

CWIS (2016) *Citywide Inclusive Sanitation: A Call to Action* [pdf], Washington, DC: World Bank <http://pubdocs.worldbank.org/en/589771503512867370/Citywide-Inclusive-Sanitation.pdf> [accessed 27 November 2017].

Elliott, M., MacDonald, M.C., Chan, T., Kearton, A., Shields, K.F., Bartram, J.K., and Hadwen, W.L. (2017) 'Multiple household water sources and their use in remote communities with evidence from Pacific Island Countries', *Water Resources Research* 53(11): 9106–17 <http://dx.doi.org/10.1002/2017WR021047>.

Hutton, G. and Chase, C. (2016) 'The knowledge base for achieving the sustainable development goal targets on water supply, sanitation and hygiene', *International Journal of Environmental Research and Public Health* 13(6): 536 <http://dx.doi.org/10.3390/ijerph13060536>.

Liddle, E.S. and Fenner, R.A. (2019) 'Using causal loop diagrams to understand handpump failure in sub-Saharan Africa', in K. Neely (ed.), *WASH and Systems Thinking*, pp. [page numbers], Rugby: Practical Action Publishing.

Manghee, S. and Poole, A. (2012) *Approaches to Conducting Political Economy Analysis in the Urban Water Sector* [pdf], Water Papers, Water Unit, Transport,

Water and ICT Department, Sustainable Development Vice Presidency <http://documents.worldbank.org/curated/en/560131468339257950/pdf/NonAsciiFileName0.pdf> [accessed 27 November 2017].

McNicholl, D. (2019) 'Applying social network analysis to WASH', in K. Neely (ed.), *WASH and Systems Thinking*, pp. [page numbers], Rugby: Practical Action Publishing.

Mills, F., Willets, J., Petterson, S., Mitchell, C., and Norman, G. (2018) 'Faecal pathogen flows and their public health risks in urban environments: a proposed approach to inform sanitation planning', *International Journal of Environmental Research and Public Health* 15(2): 181 <https://doi.org/10.3390/ijerph15020181> [accessed 27 March 2018].

Mitchell, C., Abeysuriya, K., and Ross, K. (2016) 'Making pathogen hazards visible: a new heuristic to improve sanitation investment efficacy', *Waterlines* 35(2): 163–81 <http://dx.doi.org/10.3362/1756-3488.2016.014>.

Moriarty, P., Smits, S., Butterworth, J., and Franceys, R. (2013) 'Trends in rural water supply: towards a service delivery approach', *Water Alternatives* 6(3): 329–49.

Neely, K. and Walters, J. (2016) 'Using causal loop diagramming to explore the drivers of the sustained functionality of rural water services in Timor-Leste', *Sustainability* 8(1): 57 <http://dx.doi.org/10.3390/su8010057>.

Neely, K. (2019) 'Resources for systems thinking' in K. Neely (ed.), *WASH and Systems Thinking*, pp. [page numbers], Rugby: Practical Action Publishing.

Overseas Development Institute (ODI) (2012) *Political Economy Analysis for Operations in Water and Sanitation: A Guidance Note* [pdf], London: ODI <https://www.odi.org/sites/odi.org.uk/files/odi-assets/publications-opinion-files/7652.pdf> [accessed 27 November 2017].

World Health Organization (WHO) (2017) *Climate-Resilient Water Safety Plans: Managing Health Risks Associated with Climate Variability and Change* [pdf], Geneva: WHO <http://apps.who.int/iris/bitstream/10665/258722/1/9789241512794-eng.pdf> [accessed 27 November 2017].

About the authors

Jeremy Kohlitz is a Senior Research Consultant and PhD candidate at the Institute for Sustainable Futures, University of Technology Sydney. He specializes in WASH service delivery in Pacific Island settings, where he has worked and researched since 2009, and climate change impacts on WASH. He is also involved in applied research projects in rural and urban water and sanitation across the wider Asia-Pacific region. Jeremy's PhD research investigates the application and integration of different climate change impact paradigms for rural water services. He holds an MSc in Water and Waste Engineering from the Water, Engineering and Development Centre at Loughborough University.

Naomi Carrard is a Research Principal at the Institute for Sustainable Futures, University of Technology Sydney, specializing in applied research to inform policy and practice in WASH in Asia and the Pacific regions. Naomi has qualifications in Environmental Law and Geography and 15 years' experience working in WASH, water resource management, and development effectiveness. Her research spans urban and rural water and sanitation subsectors, working in partnership with governments and civil society towards sustainable service delivery and progressive realization of the human rights to water and sanitation. She is part of the Making Rights Real consortium and the author of a widely used framework for evaluating gender equality outcomes from WASH interventions. Current research activities explore private enterprise and civil society roles in water and sanitation service delivery, progressing gender and social inclusion through WASH programming, climate-resilient services in urban and rural areas, and application of the planetary-boundaries framework to inform more sustainable and equitable WASH.

Dr Tim Foster is a Chancellor's Postdoctoral Research Fellow at the Institute for Sustainable Futures at the University of Technology Sydney. His research examines the sustainability of rural water supplies in low- and middle-income countries. Tim has been involved in both the implementation and evaluation of rural WASH and public health programmes in numerous countries across Asia and Africa.

CHAPTER 6
Bureaucracy, WASH, and systems thinking

Chris Brown

Abstract

For the adoption of systems thinking to be successful in the WASH sector, donors and policymakers need to adjust their approaches. This is often difficult due to the rigidity of the current funding and policy design paradigm. While the need to move away from the linear reductionist principles of this paradigm is becoming more widely accepted, how to achieve this shift in thinking is often less well understood.

This chapter provides a structured roadmap through which practitioners can understand how to actually design and implement programmes that embed complex adaptive systems (CAS) principles at each level of the system. This includes the principles of designing systems based on Framed Adaptation and the concept of growing a system rather than attempting to build one. It will provide guidance on how to use adaptive programming, with high levels of embedded flexibility, to build resilient systems with strong emergent properties, and will show how the restructuring of processes and procedures within and across the full hierarchical spectrum (village up to national government) of the system can produce a transparent and accountable structure that is appropriate to the resource and capacity context in which it is being implemented.

Keywords: systems thinking, WASH, programme design, implementation

ONE OF THE ENDURING PROBLEMS of applying complexity thinking to real-world scenarios has been the difficulty faced by practitioners in translating theory into practice. In development this has been a very real issue, and while individuals such as Owen Barder (2018), Duncan Green at Oxfam (2018), Harry Jones (2011) and John Young (2008) at ODI, Michael Warner (2001), Samir Rihani (2002), and Ben Ramalingam (2008) have done tremendous work breaking down the fundamentals of complexity and applying these principles to a range of development contexts, the sector is still a long way from establishing operating principles for how to embed complexity thinking into development practice.

In order to further help development practitioners to understand the applicability of these ideas, I want to try to structure the approach in a different way. Key to this will be understanding how to look at a system holistically, and then think about each component of that system from a system-wide perspective. People are often intimidated by the subject of complexity or

http://dx.doi.org/10.3362/9781780447483.006

overawed by the scale of the thinking and the alienness of the language, yet in reality the concepts are relatively simple to grasp. The challenge is less an intellectual one than one of perspective. What is most important is the ability to think intuitively about how a system really works, how systems can best adapt and evolve, and what can and cannot work in the real world.

By this point in the book, you should have a pretty good understanding of the characteristics of Complex Adaptive Systems (CAS) and be beginning to recognize some of the system behaviour discussed within your own work context. Once you have reached this point you are probably asking how all of these pieces fit together and whether it is possible to apply this system thinking to influence the behaviour and outcomes within the systems in which you work. This is the critical question for practitioners at all levels, but particularly for those working within donor organizations and NGOs that are engaged in policy and programme design.

At the core of development is the idea of improving systems, of restructuring processes in an effort to achieve long-term sustainability. CAS theory has a role to play in helping us achieve this goal, by helping us move away from the linear reductionist principles that have for a long time governed the funding and policy design paradigm.

The reality is that we are dealing with very complex problems within hugely complex operating environments populated by equally complex agents (stakeholders). In such highly adaptive social systems the multitude of interactions occurring between agents across each level of the system hierarchy are constantly in a state of feedback and reactive and adaptive flux, producing a diverse set of emergent behaviours that when observed as a whole, 'becomes not only more than, but very different, from the sum of its parts' (Anderson, 1972: 395). This non-linear emergence is what makes complex systems so difficult to predict from a behavioural point of view (Miller and Page, 2007) and is what has inadvertently led to the dependency on the reductionist approaches historically adopted within the development sector.

Under the reductionist approach, development actors are forced into looking at complex problems in oversimplified or deconstructed ways that help make implementation a simpler task (Figure 6.1). Within this perspective, complex agents are viewed as 'rational actors', often disregarding that this does not mean 'reasonable actors' (i.e. in reality agents will act with self-interest and often act in a way that undermines the interests of the system as a whole).

While this approach makes the social-engineering components of development processes easier to design, manage, and measure, it does little for the actual efficacy of the programming.

The reason for this is that by taking this approach we are disregarding key elements of the system, thereby removing our ability to understand its true mechanics, and therefore the means by which we can best influence positive emergent behaviour.

A CAS approach looks to use similar development tools to those you are accustomed to using under the reductionist approach, but in a very different

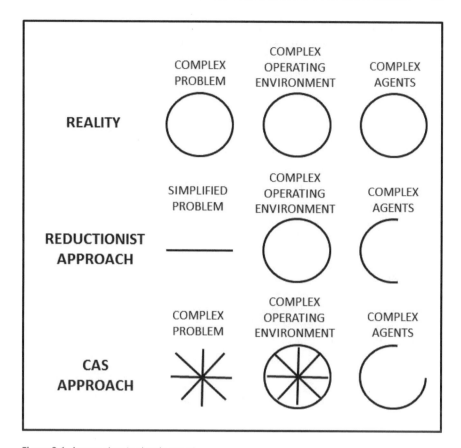

Figure 6.1 Approaches to development

way. The approach to problem identification adopts Einstein's view that 'Everything should be made *as simple as possible, but no simpler.*' This means we should not be oversimplifying problems simply to make them easier to understand or solve; instead, we should be breaking them down to their interconnected component parts to really understand the network of connections and mechanics of the processes that contribute to, or detract from, the overall health of the system. This interconnectivity helps us map the networks of interactions that occur between agents and levels of hierarchy, breaking down the linearity that has historically limited our ability to see and understand the broader mechanics of the system.

The same can be applied to the operating environment, where an attempt to really understand the dynamics of the context helps us to understand the key pillars of influence within the system that can be strengthened or coerced to create a better enabling environment for positive outcomes to occur. By doing this we are able to create an environment in which hundreds of highly interrelated simplified processes can be successfully carried out by agents with limited resources, and in which agents, while still operating in a self-interested way, are more likely to produce behaviour that also positively impacts the systemic whole.

As a theoretical concept this type of approach has a strong historical grounding in the thinking around resilience and complexity in ecology (Holling, 1973; Asokan et al., 2017) and this ecological viewpoint is helpful in understanding how to actually implement this type of thinking. Core to this approach is the idea of *growing* a system rather than trying to *build* one. Within the development context I refer to this as 'framed adaptation', the principle of which is the creation of a framework within the enabling environment, within which processes can best adapt and evolve to work within the context, skill base, and resource base available. This is not a new idea; Norberg and Cumming highlighted two key approaches to building capacity and resilience into social, environmental, and economic systems, namely:

1. Learning to identify the right signals and embed the appropriate response capacity in efficient institutional frameworks; and
2. Nurturing the capacity to adapt to change and transformations (Norberg and Cumming, 2008: 283).

This idea of nurturing development rather than engineering it was also outlined very clearly by the economist and philosopher Friedrich Hayek in his 1974 Nobel acceptance speech, in which he said:

> If man is not to do more harm than good in his efforts to improve the social order, he will have to learn that in this, as in all other fields where essential complexity of an organized kind prevails, he cannot acquire the full knowledge which would make mastery of the events possible. He will therefore have to use what knowledge he can achieve, not to shape the results as the craftsman shapes his handiwork, but rather to cultivate a growth by providing the appropriate environment, in the manner in which the gardener does this for his plants (Hayek, 1974).

It is also reflected in many other sectors. A very similar thought process is described by Eric Raymond in his book *The Cathedral and the Bazaar* (2001) in which he breaks down the difference between top-down and bottom-up approaches to free software design. The Cathedral model represents a closed-door approach to development, while in the Bazaar model, the source code is publicly available as part of a self-regulating community approach to software development that produces a more efficient, resilient, and organically grown output. This example is also very pertinent to dealing with the state of dynamic flux that exists in all CAS. The equilibrium that is so frequently sought in conventional development approaches is widely agreed not to exist in CAS. There is no equilibrium to achieve. Instead the system is seen to be constantly shifting and changing in response to local and system-wide influences and perturbations, and so we need an approach that allows for trial and error and the ability to learn and adapt quickly to the constant changes within the system. Traditionally, development actors have sought to find singular solutions to complex problems, rather than focusing on creating a flexible operating environment within which agents and processes can adapt and evolve on a natural trajectory towards more optimized behaviour.

Following this type of approach allows us to grow systems that are resilient and have high levels of embedded redundancy and flexibility, as well as in-built feedback mechanisms that allow processes and procedures within the system to adapt and evolve organically in response to emerging issues. These are the fundamental principles behind adaptive programming, and when done correctly this mirrors the ecology-based thinking that more closely resembles growing system components rather than building them. This has huge benefits, particularly in relation to stakeholder (agent) engagement and participation, and context-specific design, which will in turn lead to more positive system behaviour and emergent outcomes.

To understand what this looks like from a real-world perspective, we need to look at the working context. For the sake of explanation I want to break this down into two distinct components: the *enabling* environment and the *operating* environment.

Figure 6.2 shows a simplified framework for the enabling and operating environments within a given context. At this stage a simplified model is sufficient because we simply want to identify key drivers within each schema. Within the diagram each layer operates within the framework of the schema above, and the aim here is to identify the key elements or pillars within each schema that have the most significant direct and indirect impact on the desired outcome you are trying to achieve.

Key to making this approach work in the real world is the realization that CAS are 'self-organizing systems'. By this we mean that systems naturally move away from states of entropy, or disorder, to very different organized states, driven by the adaptive behaviour that emerges from interactions at the

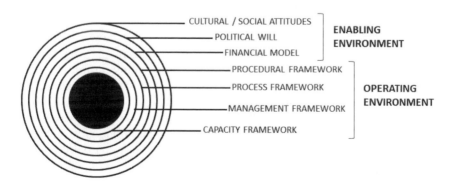

Figure 6.2 Enabling and operating environment onion

agent level. This is the principle of 'emergence', and within this principle it is important to understand that there is no adaptation by the system itself; the system level adaptation and emergent behaviour that we witness is driven by individual and collective adaptive behaviour at the agent level.

This is significant, because for agent-level adaptation to occur some level of cooperation needs to be present. In this context cooperation refers to the unspoken, but universally understood, high-level rules of operation that agents generally adhere to within social systems (Axelrod, 1984). A good example of this can be seen on any highway, where individual agents (vehicles) follow their own trajectories at varying speeds with relatively few collisions, by all following a few basic rules of operation.

If we apply this principle back to the development context, it should therefore be possible to nurture system environments, on multiple levels of the operational hierarchy, to contain the essential elements for growth, and the requisite rules of operation, to prompt the emergence of self-organizing behaviour in the system as a whole. There will of course be natural variation within this, but the combination of positive inputs, active feedback mechanisms, and an adaptive approach to programming that allows for constant adjustment and reiteration, means that the likelihood of the agents' behaviour producing emergent outcomes that have a positive impact on both the system and its agents should be significantly increased.

To provide some real-world context to this I want to explain this process through the example of the work that the UK Department for International Development (DFID) is doing with the Ministry of Water and Irrigation (MoWI) in Tanzania, to show how their use of adaptive programming and performance-based financing has helped transform the management of the rural water sector. In 2014, DFID Tanzania had a clear vision of establishing a 'Payments by Results' (PbR) programme in combination with a strong adaptive programming approach to improve service delivery and sustainability in the rural water sector in Tanzania. What was interesting about this programme from the start was that DFID was choosing to adopt a frequently challenged financing model with a very innovative (and unproven) approach to flexible and adaptive programming, the principles of which mirror a lot of the fundamentals of CAS thinking.

As a country programme DFID Tanzania already had a very good understanding of the context of the rural water sector in Tanzania, having worked closely with MoWI for many years, but for the programme to succeed it was important to identify the key drivers that would most influence change within the sector. Reviews of various processes and systems within the Ministry and the broader rural water sector highlighted two key 'pillars' that were identified as being essential foundations for success in the programme: namely, the improvement of data culture (and the poor quality of water point-related data) and the engagement of government to increase the level of political will to address rural water point sustainability issues.

These may sound like fairly obvious and universal issues to address, but in the context of the Tanzanian rural water sector generally, and the PbR programme specifically, these two points of focus opened up a whole spectrum of other areas of influence and knock-on effects that allowed the PbR programme to have a significant impact on the evolution of the system.

If we look at a basic causal loop diagram (Figure 6.3) of how these two 'pillar' processes interact to influence the desired end goal of improved sustainability, we see that as elements of the enabling environment, they are critical in nurturing the development of the greater transparency, accountability, and operational efficiency that were lacking within the sector.

Understanding these drivers allowed DFID and MoWI to look at, and map (Figure 6.4), a number of actionable drivers within each of these elements, that would in turn foster greater levels of cooperation and therefore adaptation across the various levels of the sector hierarchy: ministry, zone, region, district, ward, and village.

If we look at these factors from the enabling and operating environment perspective we can see how these elements interact across the two environments to create the foundations for a more positive, cooperative, and operationally efficient service delivery system.

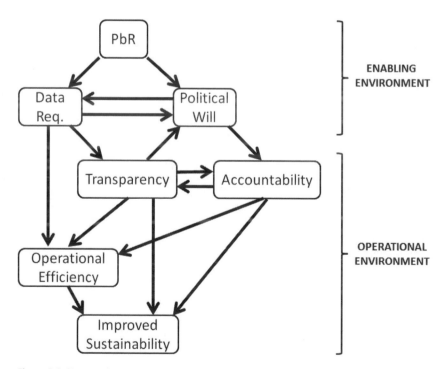

Figure 6.3 Network interactions of the key 'pillars' of PbR

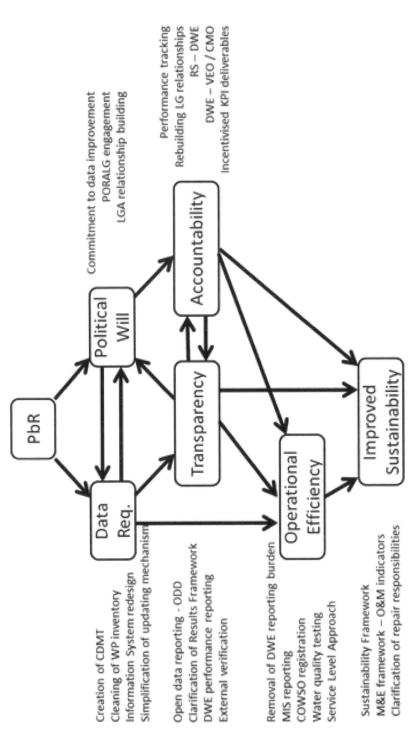

Abbreviations

CDMT: Central Data Management Team; CMO: community management organization; COWSO: community owned water supply organization; DWE: district water engineer; KPI: key performance indicator; LGA: local government authority; M&E: monitoring & evaluation; MIS: management information system; O&M: operations & maintenance; ODD: open data dashboard; PbR: payments by results;
PORALG: President's Office for Regional and Local Government; RS: regional secretary; VEO: village executive officer; WP: water point

Figure 6.4 Sub-level actionable drivers within the rural water sector in Tanzania

Enabling environment

Cultural

The primary issue was the crisis of data, namely a lack of data culture, expertise, and procedural structure. DFID knew that without improving the data quality and reporting, effective operation and maintenance of water infrastructure would be impossible, and so engaging government to establish the requisite level of political will for change was paramount.

Political will

Reciprocally, this was key to establishing a commitment to improving data. It also fostered the establishment of the Central Data Management Team (CDMT) within the MoWI, tasked with managing the improvement of data, and the embedding of Technical Assistance within the Rural Water Supply Directorate (RWSD). Finally, for water-point sustainability to be improved, the political engagement of the President's Office for Regional Administration and Local Government (PORALG) needed to occur, so that Local Government Authority (LGA) cooperation could be obtained. This has helped foster increased accountability within government, which in turn has laid the platform for greater transparency of process and a more self-policing culture within the rural water sector.

Financial model

PbR uses incentive-based payments to drive improvements to reporting frequency, data quality, and ultimately operations and maintenance as outputs. As a financing scheme its primary impact has been in nurturing government engagement and not in directly incentivizing output. This was a surprise to many but it fits very neatly into the CAS narrative of influencing the enabling environment to drive positive change to internal processes and behaviour within the system. This is a very clear example of 'framed adaptation'.

Operating environment

Procedural framework

The creation of the CDMT and the engagement of senior management within MoWI has led to wholesale changes in the procedural structure for data reporting and management, approaches to Community Management, Community Owned Water Supply Organizations (COWSO) engagement and registration, the restructuring of the monitoring and evaluation framework to include a new set of operations and maintenance indicators, and the release of a restructured Sustainability Framework outlining a cooperative approach to future sustainability of water service delivery.

Process framework

This involved the simplification and reduction of LGA reporting and inventory management processes to help District Water Engineers to manage processes more efficiently. It also effected the introduction of water-quality testing criteria at a national level and the restructuring of reporting indicators to reflect a service level approach, rather than the traditional 'access to water' paradigm that misrepresents the actual level of service received by users.

Management framework

The direct support of management processes through the establishment of a technical adviser dedicated to full-time RWSD management support has directly led to sector-wide performance monitoring across the whole of the RWSD.

Capacity framework

Processes have been restructured to fit the capacity and resources of MoWI and local government staff, with a focus on a change in approach to understanding the system as a whole rather than as a series of detached non-interacting components. This has helped agents within every tier of the system better understand how their direct actions influence the broader outcomes of the system, thereby positively influencing behaviour.

Critically, DFID deferred the start of the programme for two years running, until the government had made sufficient commitment to improving data quality for the programme to be implementable. While on the surface this was tied very closely to the data pillar, in reality it was key to ensuring that the requisite level of political will was in place to take processes forward.

Two years on, and it is still a little early to really see the impact of the changes at a system level, but the start of agent-level behaviour change is already evident. The stripping down and simplification of reporting requirements has led to an increase in the response rates of LGAs in submitting their monthly water-point inventory status updates, from 26 per cent to 99 per cent in the first year of the CDMT being operational. An additional benefit that arose from the changes made at process level was that almost 30,000 water points that were missing from the national inventory have been recovered, along with their full set of indicators and geo-referencing. Interestingly, these changes are largely by-products of broader procedural changes around the need to use this data for transparent reporting, and the requirement to openly account for data that is reported, both of which have had positive feedback effects on data quality improvement and political commitment to the process. In addition to this, the restructuring of the monitoring and evaluation and sustainability frameworks has led to the rollout of additional operations and maintenance indicators that for the first time will be part of a single monthly status report from District Water Engineers that will allow local and national government to track service level instead of just measuring access to water.

Furthermore, the re-establishment of severed links between the MoWI and the regional and LGA administrations has started to create a better management and accountability structure across all tiers of governance, and this is now being expanded to include village level executive officers and community management organizations. The kickbacks from this should be increased cooperation between tiers of government, improved reporting and accuracy of data, and greater accountability as communities are provided with an audience for their issues and feedback. Once these processes become embedded, we should start to see changes in the way water points are managed, which should in turn influence sustainability levels over time.

On the national level, improved cooperation through the burgeoning inter-ministerial relationships that exist between MoWI, PORALG, and other peripheral ministries such as the Ministry of Lands and the National Bureau of Statistics has helped streamline procedural and process level changes across local government. The feedback from these changes (seen through improved reporting and data quality, increased communication between stakeholder groups, and improvements in transparency and accountability within government) all serve to further strengthen inter-governmental relations, because positive outcomes breed further positive enforcing behaviour, which in turn increase the likelihood of further positive outcomes at an emergent level.

What has been an interesting side effect of this approach is that while financial incentives have been a key driver in garnering political engagement in high level government structures, they have proven less of a driver at local government level than the internal governmental pressure that has been driven by increased levels of transparency and accountability within government. So the interconnectedness and feedback mechanisms that exist within the enabling environment are already becoming self-evident.

This 'framed adaptation' approach to manipulating the enabling environment as a way of nurturing cooperation and positive emergent behaviour works because it helps provide a balance between controlling 'limiters' and a free-market adaptive culture. This creates a better operating environment within which actors are more likely to make positive decisions and therefore positive emergent outcomes are more likely to occur (despite there being a highly non-linear relationship between them). Hopefully this case study helps to illustrate just how systems can be designed and managed in a real-world context, by showing how the nurturing of simple targeted process mechanisms within the system can lead to positive emergent behaviour over time.

References

Anderson, P. (1972) 'More Is different', *Science* 177(4047): 393–6.

Asokan, V.A., Yarime, M., and Esteban, M. (2017) 'Introducing flexibility to complex, resilient socio-ecological systems: a comparative analysis of economics, flexible manufacturing systems, evolutionary biology, and supply chain management', *Sustainability Open Access Journal* 9(7): 1091 <http://dx.doi.org/10.3390/su9071091>.

Axelrod, R. (1984) *The Evolution of Cooperation*, New York, NY: Basic Books.

Barder, O. (2018) *The Implications of Complexity for Development – Owen Barder* [online], Center For Global Development <https://www.cgdev.org/media/implications-complexity-development-owen-barder> [accessed January 2018].

Green, D. (2018) *Complexity: From Poverty to Power* [online] https://oxfamblogs.org/fp2p/tag/complexity/ [accessed January 2018].

Hayek, F. (1974) *Friedrich August von Hayek – Prize Lecture* [online] <https://www.nobelprize.org/nobel_prizes/economic-sciences/laureates/1974/hayek-lecture.html> [accessed January 2018].

Holling, C.S. (1973) 'Resilience and stability of ecological systems', *Annual Review of Ecology and Systematics* 4: 1–23.

Jones, H. (2011) *Taking Responsibility for Complexity: How Implementation Can Achieve Results in the Face of Complex Problems*, ODI Working Paper 330, London, UK: Overseas Development Institute.

Miller, J. and Page, S. (2007) *Complex Adaptive Systems: an Introduction to Computational Models of Social Life*, Princeton, NJ: Princeton University Press.

Norberg, J. and Cumming, G. (2008) *Complexity Theory for a Sustainable Future*, New York: Columbia University Press.

Ramalingam, B. (2008) *Aid on the Edge of Chaos*, Oxford, UK: Oxford University Press.

Ramalingam, B., Jones, H., Reba, T., and Young, J. (2008) *Exploring the Science of Complexity: Ideas and Implications for Development and Humanitarian Efforts*, ODI Working Paper 285, London, UK: Overseas Development Institute.

Raymond, E. (2001) *The Cathedral and the Bazaar*, Boston, MA: O'Reilly Media.

Rihani, S. (2002) 'Implications of adopting a complexity framework for development', *Progress in Development Studies* 2(2): 133–43 <https://doi.org/10.1191/1464993402ps033pr>.

Warner, M. (2001) *Complex Problems...Negotiated Solutions: The Practical Applications of Chaos and Complexity Theory to Community-based Natural Resource Management*, ODI Working Paper 146, London, UK: Overseas Development Institute.

About the author

Chris Brown is a development consultant specializing in integrated risk management, resilience building, and monitoring and evaluation, with a focus on the WASH sector. He is also the founder and director of WEL Group Consulting. He has an MSc in Environment and Development and over 12 years' experience working on a range of projects for both governments and organizations, including DFID, IRC, the Red Cross Climate Centre, Save the Children, LSHTM, World Vision, and WaterAid. He has extensive experience in the design and implementation of monitoring, evaluation, and mapping processes, particularly in the use of ICT for monitoring and in the design of comprehensive process cycles that incorporate effective and sustainable mechanisms for the collection, analysis, and updating of data inventories. He is also a specialist in the application and integration of complex adaptive systems theory into conventional development approaches to create more sustainable and resilient systems within which development processes can more effectively operate and evolve.

CHAPTER 7

Learning for adaptive management: using systems thinking tools to inform knowledge and learning approaches

Melita Grant and Juliet Willetts

Abstract

This chapter explores how learning theory and systems thinking tools can help WASH organizations select the most appropriate processes and tools to facilitate learning, leverage greatest WASH impacts, and support their staff to optimize their learning potential. We draw on two key systems thinking tools: the Cynefin framework developed by David Snowden and Donella Meadows' leverage points. The Cynefin framework can be used to help actors identify what kind of WASH situation an organization is operating within, and which learning tools and processes might be most useful for each situation. The concept of 'leverage points' can support a process of stepping back to consider the kinds of changes needed and intended, which 'levers' could create such changes in a WASH situation, and which learning processes are best suited to a particular leverage point. By using these tools from the outset, organizations can make informed, strategic decisions about where to place scarce resources for knowledge and learning to increase leverage, and maximize WASH outcomes. This chapter concludes that learning can be a key driver of sustainability transformation and impact, but only if inequitable power dynamics are challenged, critical thinking is employed, and learning is truly shared and applied to real-world problems.

Keywords: learning, knowledge, adaptive management, systems thinking, WASH, civil society organizations

THE GLOBAL WASH SECTOR has embraced learning as an important component of its monitoring and evaluation processes, and considers learning to be essential to adaptive management and improved practice. However, WASH organizations face challenges in facilitating learning in the most effective and timely manner, and in using the scarce resources available for this purpose. This chapter explores how learning theory and systems thinking tools can help WASH organizations target the right processes and tools to support learning, and how these tools can enable organizations to support their staff to optimize their learning potential.

http://dx.doi.org/10.3362/9781780447483.007

The lack of success of many WASH interventions has partly been a result of knowledge gaps and failures in the uptake of learning. For example, a systematic review of WASH interventions to control cholera found that there was a distinct gap in knowledge about which interventions were most appropriate in particular contexts (Taylor et al., 2015). Failures are also widely understood to be a result of a historical focus on technology, at the expense of more integrated approaches aimed at influencing the enabling environment (i.e. the political, legal, institutional, financial, educational, technical, and social conditions) (Tilley et al., 2014). A study on learning within and between WASH civil society organizations found that barriers to learning included concerns about reputation (if failures were to become public), funding issues (lack of resources), donor perceptions (in terms of fears of exposing what did not go to plan), and simply being extremely busy and overworked (Grant et al., 2016: 19). The WASH sector has an opportunity to use systems concepts to address these barriers and failures. For example, an explicit focus on feedback loops could promote learning throughout programmes, and this could in turn increase the effectiveness of WASH interventions.

It has been recognized that the Sustainable Development Goals need to be addressed in an integrated way, and this requires practitioners to explore different approaches to programme design, delivery, and evaluation (Stafford-Smith et al., 2016). To help them to adopt integrated approaches, practitioners need examples of learning frameworks, and of frameworks that will enable them to identify feedbacks between sectors. Critical pedagogical literature offers a series of frameworks and examples of how embedding learning into projects can lead to improved conduct and self-reflection (Deakin Crick, 2012; Senge, 1990). In a complementary way, the extensive use of the theory and practice of soft-systems thinking to deal with sustainable development problems also provides ways of linking issues in the WASH sector with broader development targets. In this chapter, we explore how different learning and systems theories can contribute to improving the way the WASH sector embeds knowledge and learning processes within its design, implementation, and evaluation.

Learning is fundamental to systems thinking, adaptive management, and ecological and social sustainability (König, 2018), and by extension, to all WASH practices and processes. Learning supports individuals and organizations to better understand the contexts they are working within, to test and trial approaches, to make decisions, and to see the short- and long-term impacts of their interventions. One learning framework of relevance to the WASH sector is the one developed by Deakin Crick (2012), which stresses the importance of a learner's purpose. It emphasizes that learning will be most effective if people are able to identify their own learning needs, and if they learn while doing through real-world experiences (Deakin Crick, 2012; Deakin Crick et al., 2012). This process, referred to as a 'learning journey', has been found to be more powerful if it is integrated with the flow of daily work, applied to solving authentic challenges, and built around networks and relationships, while tapping into peoples' core values (Deakin Crick, 2012).

This framework echoes the learning theory of Paulo Freire, whose seminal work *Pedagogy of the Oppressed* advocated for people to learn with each other through dialogue, action, and critical reflection. Opportunities to learn in these ways are offered in organizational environments referred to as learning organizations, in which people are supported to expand their capacities, and 'where people are continually learning how to learn together' (Senge, 1990: 3).

In addition to drawing on these learning frameworks, in this chapter we discuss two key systems thinking tools which may help the WASH sector to inform knowledge and learning approaches: the Cynefin framework (Snowden, 2005) and Meadows' leverage points (Meadows, 1999, 2008). The Cynefin framework can be used to help actors identify what kind of WASH situation an organization is operating within, and which learning tools and processes might be most useful for each situation. The Cynefin framework (Snowden, 2002, 2005; Snowden and Boone, 2007) identified four domains (see Figure 7.3) that can help practitioners with decision-making and learning by stimulating reflection about the level of complexity of a situation before they develop specific intervention strategies.

The concept of 'leverage points' developed by Meadows (1999, 2008) can support a process of stepping back to consider the kinds of changes needed and intended, which 'levers' could be used to create specific changes in a WASH situation, and which learning processes are best suited to enabling a particular leverage point to be accessed. In this chapter, we show how leverage points can be used to identify the purpose of learning within WASH organizations. We examine the kinds of decisions WASH sector actors should make to elicit the types of changes they want to see, moving towards the ultimate goal of universal access to safe water and sanitation. The ways in which WASH organizations decide to work towards this ultimate goal are varied, and they reflect their value systems and their underlying theories of change. When it comes to developing strategies, Meadows' (1999, 2008) 12 leverage points provide a useful and practical perspective on the effectiveness that strategies have in creating positive learning processes. Meadows is of particular relevance given that she was one of the first to apply systems thinking concepts to sustainability issues, of which WASH is one.

These two systems thinking tools can be used by WASH organizations to develop overarching strategies, and to support theories of change, but in this chapter we focus on *learning processes* that occur within and between organizations. We examine how organizations can use these tools to evolve in order to carry out effective work and adaptively manage their policies and programmes. Adaptive management is the process of learning by doing, and adjusting courses of action through learning (Holling, 1978). The WASH sector is increasingly using adaptive management approaches in order to respond to dynamic environments and improve the sustainability of its investments.

Together, the Cynefin framework and Meadows' leverage points provide useful ways of thinking about learning processes, about how to choose which tools are best suited to particular systems, and about how to work with

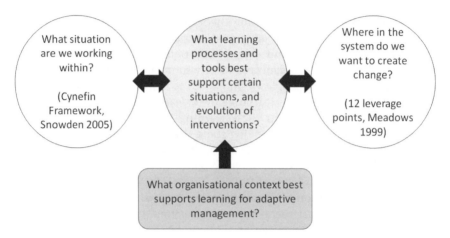

Figure 7.1 Key questions and systems thinking tools canvassed in this chapter

a system to elicit improvements. Together, they help answer the question: 'What learning processes and tools best support different WASH situations and the evolution of WASH interventions?' – the key question addressed in this chapter (see Figure 7.1). The organizational context, or the environment in which learning takes place, influences the quality and nature of the learning that occurs, and hence it is also included in Figure 7.1.

In this chapter we draw on examples from the WASH sector, both in relation to types of changes or interventions that organizations seek to create, and the types of knowledge and learning products and processes that can support them. We present case studies and examples that demonstrate how the WASH sector is implementing learning programmes and initiatives, and how these relate to the systems thinking tools presented in the chapter. We first examine recent research related to 'knowledge and learning' in the WASH sector conducted by the authors of this chapter (Grant et al., 2016) as background context for the application of the systems thinking tools.

Knowledge and learning in the WASH sector

The global WASH sector has developed knowledge and learning initiatives over many decades to improve its effectiveness in policy and practice, and ultimately to increase the number of people with safe and accessible water, sanitation, and hygiene services (da Silva-Wells and Verhoeven, 2013). More recently, time and effort dedicated to learning within the sector has been boosted by financial support for sector-wide, regional, and organizational learning processes. Examples include the Civil Society WASH Fund supported by the Australian Aid programme; research and learning initiatives of Water and Sanitation for the Urban Poor and Stichting Nederlandse Vrijwilligers (SNV) Development Organization; and investments in learning by the Gates

Foundation. Well-known and highly utilized communities of practice have developed and continue to expand. They include the Sustainable Sanitation Alliance (SuSanA) and the Rural Water Supply Network (RWSN).

Learning occurs within the WASH sector at different levels: individually, as people learn and grow in their own professions and roles; between and among individuals; between organizations; as a part of engagement between WASH organizations and the communities they work in; between donors and the organizations they fund; between governments and research institutions and WASH civil society organizations; and within local, regional, and global communities of practice.

Despite growing attention to the *learning* component of monitoring, evaluation, and learning, the research conducted by the authors of this chapter found that the extent to which learning is considered core business varied across the sector (Grant et al., 2016). The same study found that support for learning has been influenced by a range of factors including organizational learning culture, funding for learning, donor influence, and leaders' perceptions of the role of learning within the organization.

Other research on the organizational context that facilitates learning and effectiveness has found that the leadership of an organization drives its learning culture, and that learning depends on leaders' commitment to training, learning, and experimentation (Whatley, 2013). This was supported by the Grant et al. (2016) study which found that in addition to leadership, other important elements of WASH civil society organizations' (CSOs') learning culture included time and space for reflection, utilizing monitoring and evaluation data, and seeking opportunities to learn from peers and from failure. Visscher et al. (2006) suggest that the characteristics of a learning organization include that they are future driven, have free exchange of information, are committed to learning from top management, devote time to learning, value diversity, foster a climate of openness, and encourage people to learn from mistakes. These insights provide valuable guidance for how the WASH sector can create learning environments.

Learning methods

Moving from the organizational learning environment to focus on specific learning processes and tools, we now briefly present findings from Grant et al. (2016) regarding respondents' preferences and their feedback on the effectiveness of different approaches. A wide variety of approaches to learning are used in the WASH sector. These include various modes of face-to-face and online knowledge capture and sharing, including conferences, learning alliances, webinars, and e-discussions. Each approach uses various forms of documentation. In 17 interviews and 82 surveys, the respondents in Grant et al.'s (2016) study reported that learning from peers and learning on the job were the forms of learning that led to the greatest levels of improved practice among WASH practitioners (Figure 7.2). Forms of peer-based learning included learning from

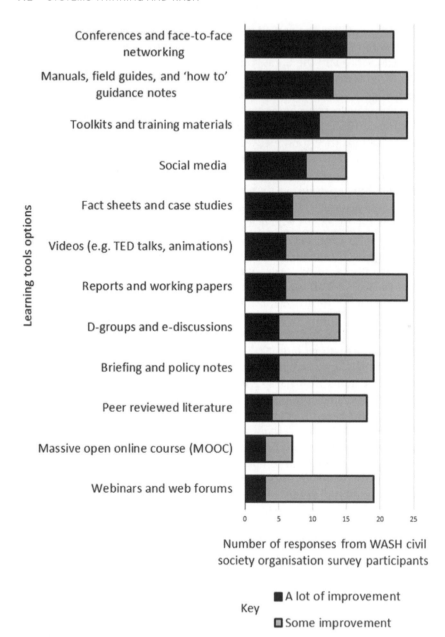

Figure 7.2 Learning tools and products considered to have led to improved practice within WASH CSOs (self-reported by WASH CSO respondents)
Note: for simplicity, responses of 'don't know' and 'not at all' have been omitted.

workshops, conferences, and networks, as well as learning exchanges within and between organizations.

These results highlight the perceived value of face-to-face engagement as well as manuals and field-guides. The results can be both explained and interrogated further by examining the two systems thinking frameworks and how they might inform WASH sector organizations' choices of learning processes and tools.

Applying systems thinking tools to the WASH sector for learning and adaptive management

In this section we describe two selected systems thinking frameworks and their relevance to WASH sector learning processes and tools. Due to the wide range of lineages, methodologies, and tools of systems thinking that have been developed over the past 100 years, it is often difficult and confusing for practitioners to choose the most appropriate approaches for dealing with WASH sector challenges. It is also important to note that many WASH practitioners draw on systems thinking without using the term, or without drawing on specific theoretical tools and frameworks. However, without understanding the foundations of the concepts upon which systems thinking is based, opportunities for deeper synergies and for embedding learning within other processes, such as developing theories of change, could be missed. Therefore, a number of key concepts used in systems thinking that are important to consider in light of this chapter are shown in Table 7.1, along with examples from the WASH sector.

Systems thinking tools useful for developing knowledge and learning initiatives

The way in which we perceive and produce knowledge could be a key lever for sustainability transformation (Abson et al., 2017: 35). Knowledge, and the way it is used in society, can influence system leverage points (where small changes can have big impacts), and therefore it is important to understand how knowledge flows through a system. Moreover, by challenging and questioning how knowledge is produced and used in learning processes, we can identify gaps in knowledge, the limitations of existing knowledge processes, and the socially constructed assumptions that may be barriers to transformations towards sustainability (Abson et al., 2017). Abson et al. (2017) call for new collaborative and diverse forms of knowledge production to underpin and drive transformational sustainability interventions. Given the diverse social-ecological factors underpinning many sustainability problems (including WASH problems), we need to integrate different types of knowledge (Abson et al., 2017), and this is a process that can be supported through transdisciplinary approaches (Wickson et al., 2006). In the WASH sector, the types of knowledge that need to be integrated include (but are not limited to) knowledge from communities,

Table 7.1 Key concepts used in systems thinking, and examples from the WASH sector to illustrate them

Systems thinking concept	Definition	Example from the WASH sector
Variable	Variables are the changeable parts of the system that affect stocks (resources) and flows (the amounts of the stocks) (Arnold and Wade, 2015).	Number of latrines, taps, wells, and piped water connections.
Boundary setting	The process in which the observer(s) define the borders of the system. Boundaries can be biophysical, but also social, such as power and cultural boundaries (Ulrich and Reynolds, 2010).	1. Defining the boundary (for example) at the provincial level with a focus on private piped water system entrepreneurs. 2. The power held over water allocation and how this influences water access.
Positive feedback loops	A positive (or reinforcing) feedback loop is self-reinforcing and results in a vicious or virtuous cycle. 'Positive feedback loops drive growth, explosion, erosion, and collapse in systems' (Meadows, 1997: 6).	Overuse of piped water systems in a context of water scarcity/shortage, without water conservation programmes and/or disincentives for unnecessary usage in place. Increased water consumption is self-reinforcing as behavioural norms are established (for example water used by hotels and industry without efficiency/demand management in place).
Negative feedback loops	Negative (or balancing) feedback loops are where an increase in one variable leads to a decrease in another, which brings the system back into stability (Open University, 2005).	Poor sanitation leading to diseases and stunted growth among children, resulting in actions taken to improve sanitation.
Leverage point	Any place within a complex adaptive system (a corporation, an economy, a living body, a city, an ecosystem) where a small shift in one thing can produce big changes in everything (Meadows, 1997).	The recognition of the relationships between WASH in schools, education outcomes, and gender equality. With adequate toilets, handwashing options, and menstrual hygiene management facilities, school attendance (particularly of girls) is boosted.

(continues)

Table 7.1 (*continued*)

Systems thinking concept	Definition	Example from the WASH sector
Emergent property/ behaviour	Emergent behaviour is behaviour of a system that does not depend on its individual parts, but on their relationships to one another. Emergent behaviour occurs as sub-systems interact (Ison, 2008).	Sustaining city-wide sanitation services requires a combination of well-functioning technologies, sustained demand, effective management, and sustainable financing, within a broader enabling regulatory and policy environment (Ross et al., 2014 in ISF-UTS and SNV, 2016).
Hard systems thinking	Discrete systems are perceived to exist, can be identified and then engineered (Checkland, 2000: S17).	A system defined as a commune-level, small-scale piped water scheme with clearly defined geographic boundaries.
Soft systems thinking	The world is complex and confusing and influenced by worldviews and human values. Through the process of inquiry and exploration, a learning system emerges (Checkland, 2000: S17).	The relationship between water and sanitation in terms of water quantity and quality, and how these sectors relate to each other.

governments, academics, the private sector, and a wide range of fields such as land-use planning, political economy, public health, engineering, ecological economics, and water resources management. In the context of learning, we argue in this chapter that it is important to link learning processes and tools with systems thinking frameworks, so that they best serve the situation that a WASH actor is working within, and so that they are tailored to suit the types of change that are being leveraged.

The next section outlines the Cynefin framework (Snowden, 2005), and provides examples of learning approaches from the WASH sector. We then present Meadows' (1999) 12 leverage points framework, also with reference to learning approaches, and the ways in which knowledge and learning can drive sustainability transformation.

WASH, learning, and the Cynefin framework

David Snowden introduced the Cynefin framework in 2005 when he published his seminal paper, 'Strategy in the context of uncertainty' (Snowden, 2005). Snowden argued that there are various levels of complexity within which organizations operate, which relate to the degree to which cause and effect are, or can be, known in a particular context. According to Snowden (2005), the degree to which 'best practice' can be replicated, the degree to which case studies can be applied to other contexts, and the degree to which experts can be used to make decisions, are all highly context-dependent. The Cynefin framework distinguishes between four domains: Simple, Complicated, Complex, and Chaotic (Snowden, 2005), as shown in Figure 7.3.

Building on the Cynefin framework, we explain each of the domains, provide examples from the WASH sector that may fit within each domain, and map the commonly used learning processes and tools that are most relevant to each domain (see Table 7.2). It should be noted that this mapping is not definitive, and that, depending on their nature, certain learning processes or tools may be applicable to different domains. Project managers and knowledge and learning staff within WASH organizations can use the mapping shown in Table 7.2 to consider which of the four domains their WASH initiative is positioned within, and therefore how they might best respond to the situation, and what kinds of learning processes and tools might be most relevant. Below we provide a more detailed explanation of each domain and the WASH learning within it.

WASH learning in the simple domain

As seen in Table 7.2, the 'simple domain' is characterized by the fact that the relationships between cause and effect exist, are known, and can be used to inform strategies to address a particular issue. In this domain, past experience can also be used to inform the strategy, and best practice can be employed.

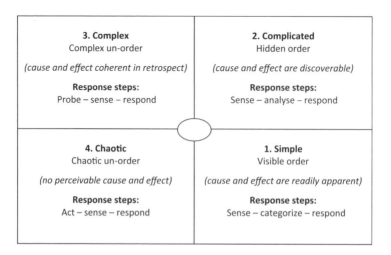

Figure 7.3 Cynefin domains
Source: Adapted from Snowden (2005: 50)

Table 7.2 Mapping the Cynefin framework against WASH sector strategies and learning processes and tools

Cynefin framework domain (Snowden, 2005)	Explanation (adapted from Snowden, 2005)	WASH sector situations	Examples of learning processes and tools commonly used in the WASH sector, loosely mapped against Cynefin framework
Simple **Response steps:** Sense – categorize – respond	The relationship between cause and effect exists and is repeatable and predictable. There are one or a few good responses to the problem or situation that are known and can be drawn upon.	• Leaks in a piped water system • Handwashing infrastructure (water/soap) in facilities (e.g. schools, hospitals, and homes) • Latrine construction	• Standard operating procedures • Best practice guidance • Plumbing regulations • Construction design guideline
Complicated **Response steps:** Sense – analyse – respond	It is clear what the problem is, and existing expertise can help make sense of it. There is agreement about what needs to be done, and although the 'how' may not be clear, the path forward is relatively uncontroversial.	• WASH facilities in schools and healthcare facilities • Construction of disability-accessible WASH facilities • Community-scale water or sanitation scheme construction	• Technical reports • Toolkits • Training materials • Manuals and 'how to' guides
Complex **Response steps:** Probe – sense – respond	There is uncertainty around the starting point and end-point of the problem, and there is no obvious preferred strategy, which means that strategies are emergent.	• Hygiene-behaviour change campaigns	• Discussion groups and e-discussions • Stakeholder engagement/consultation

(continues)

Table 7.2 (*continued*)

Cynefin framework domain (*Snowden, 2005*)	Explanation (*adapted from Snowden, 2005*)	WASH sector situations	*Examples of learning processes and tools commonly used in the WASH sector, loosely mapped against Cynefin framework*
	There are conflicting values and interests at stake, and there are complex and non-linear connections between relevant components. Delays in feedback and information flows may emerge as unintended consequences. In this context, stakeholders need to decide what is best through continued attention, learning, and negotiation.	• Clean water, sanitation, and hygiene service delivery models in rural communities or informal settlements • Financing rural water and sanitation schemes	• Real-time learning • Action research and action learning • Mini-experiments • 'Principles'-level guidance (dimensions that need thinking and attention) • Systematic reviews of available evidence
Chaotic Response steps: Act – sense – respond	Chains of cause and effect cannot be identified in the chaotic domain, and so the only way to function in this domain is to take quick action to stabilize a situation and attempt to move back into one of the other domains.	• WASH in humanitarian crisis contexts (such as cholera outbreaks, typhoons, floods) • Addressing community water needs during times of acute water scarcity/drought and/or water pollution incidents	• Humanitarian emergency response communications via social media and the traditional media, early warning systems, and stakeholder coordination systems

For example, fixing leaks is a relatively straightforward plumbing task, and although there may be a range of ways to fix the leak, there are established ways to do this, and guidelines and documented knowledge to draw on. Examples of learning tools relevant to the simple domain are standard operating procedures, best practice guidelines, and plumbing regulations. These all capture past experience and enable it to be replicated.

An example from the WASH sector of a learning process and tool that sits within the simple domain is the 'Latrine Design and Construction' workshop and manual developed by the Centre for Affordable Water and Sanitation Technology (CAWST). The workshop teaches participants to design and construct appropriate and desirable latrines for low-income communities not connected to a sewerage system (CAWST, 2014).

WASH learning in the complicated domain

In the complicated domain, there is agreement about what needs to be done. Although the 'how' may not be clear, the path forward is relatively uncontroversial. In this domain, the relationship between cause and effect is not as clear as in the simple domain, and so expert knowledge to assist analysis is required. Examples from the WASH sector that may be understood to be within the complicated domain include building WASH facilities in schools and healthcare contexts, disability-accessible WASH facilities, and community-scale water or sanitation scheme construction (Table 7.2).

In the complicated domain, learning tools such as technical reports, toolkits, training materials, manuals, and 'how to' guides can provide access to expert knowledge, but this knowledge needs to be contextualized and used in the analysis process, not directly applied in ways that are possible within the simple domain.

An example of a learning tool from the WASH sector that can be considered to be within the complicated domain is the UNICEF Sanitation Marketing Learning Series (2014). The 10 guidance notes in the series include: *Situation Analysis: How do I Know if SanMark Will Work in My Country?*; *Getting the Product 'Right': How Do We Design Affordable, Desirable Latrines that Businesses can Profitably Produce and Sell?*; and guidance on engaging with the enabling environment (UNICEF, 2014). The guidance emphasizes that programme strategies and activities must be designed to fit domestic market conditions, and decision-making frames are provided to support WASH actors' strategies when considering sanitation-marketing modalities. This tool is relevant to the complicated domain as it captures a range of existing expertise which can be used to implement sanitation marketing programmes in a range of contexts. However, this knowledge needs to be adapted to each context to suit the local conditions using appropriate expertise, as opposed to being directly replicated. In addition, complementary learning processes suitable to the complex domain may also need to be applied to enable the appropriate contextualization and adaptation of guidance tools such as the UNICEF Sanitation Marketing Learning Series (2014).

WASH learning in the complex domain

Successful management in the complex domain is dependent on deep learning processes, and stakeholders need to identify strategies together. Unlike the simple and complicated domains, there is uncertainty around the starting point and end-point of the problem, and there is no obvious preferred strategy, which means that strategies are emergent.

Examples of WASH situations that may fall within the complex domain include hygiene behaviour change campaigns, service delivery models for clean water, and sanitation and hygiene projects in rural communities and informal settlements. In these situations, there are conflicting values and interests at stake, and complex and non-linear connections between the relevant factors (Table 7.2). There are also delays in feedback and information flows, which make it necessary for stakeholders to decide what is best through continuing attention, learning, and negotiation. An example is using real-time learning tools such as those employed in the Cambodian WASH sector (see Box 7.1). Emergent properties (where the relationships between sub-systems are key to understanding a situation) are important to consider in the complex domain, as the relationships across and between sectors (for example) will influence the design and delivery of sustainable WASH services. The findings that 38 per cent of healthcare facilities worldwide do not have safe water supplies, 19 per cent do not have improved sanitation, and 35 per cent lack equipment for hand washing (WHO and UNICEF, 2015) point to situations where there is a need for this cross-sectoral approach.

In the complex domain, WASH sector actors engage in adaptive and emergent forms of learning, decision-making, and participatory action research. Relevant learning processes and tools include interactions within communities of practice, and forms of face-to-face engagement in which learning takes place through discourse, the sharing of experiences, and deliberation. In the complex domain, the relationship between cause and effect is not linear and may not have been experienced before. Therefore, manuals and 'how to' guides, for example, will not be particularly useful in this domain, given that cause and effect can only be understood in retrospect. In the complex domain, patterns emerge between the multiple and varied parts of the situation, and qualitative research and storytelling are important for identifying these emerging patterns.

Another example of a learning forum developed by the WASH sector that supports activity in the complex domain is the WASH Forum and Sanitation Working Group in Timor-Leste (and similar groups that exist in other country contexts). These groups focus on information sharing between government and civil society actors, including the sharing of current project plans and implementation details, as well as key areas of learning, success, and failure.

Box 7.1 WASH learning in Cambodia

An example of a learning tool that fits well within the complex domain is the real-time learning programme of the Cambodia Rural Sanitation and Hygiene Improvement Programme (CRSHIP). Introduced in 2016, the CRSHIP introduced a programme to provide opportunities for continuous reflection and learning in the context of adaptive programming (J. Dumpert, personal communication, 2017). Eleven civil society organizations and a range of government bodies at the national, provincial, and district levels were involved in the programme, supported by a small team of programme managers and field support staff (J. Dumpert, 2017). Initial meetings with project partners revealed that they preferred visual and 'learning-by-doing' methods of communication and learning tools, which is why these learning modalities were chosen (Padilla and Dumpert, 2017). The programme was based on systems thinking concepts and utilized a number of learning processes, including a closed group Facebook platform, quarterly 'pause and reflect' meetings which brought practitioners together, and the development of case studies which emerged from engagement on the Facebook group. The programme developed extensive qualitative data related to real-time experiences, questions, and insights from programme participants.

Key elements of the learning approach included the use of incentives, real-time feedback on participation, reflection papers, and making explicit the connections between learning experience, monitoring, evaluation and learning, and adaptive management. Incentives were provided to project participants to join in the conversation on Facebook, which resulted in high levels of engagement and practitioner contribution. Incentives included rewards and public praise, and expectations were set by donors in funding agreements. Real-time feedback to participants about their engagement also helped to catalyse action and involvement in the forum. The project managers coded each post in the Facebook conversations, and identified areas where knowledge resulted in adaptive management processes. These adaptations included, for example, changes in programme design or delivery as a result of the learning that occurred. Reflection papers were drawn from this data, capturing the overall learnings from the process. This learning approach is an example of one that fits within the complex domain because of the real-time learning dimension of the initiative, and the way in which it helped implementers, managers, and partners to recognize trends and patterns, and respond to challenges as projects were being implemented.

WASH learning in the chaotic domain

The chaotic domain is characterized by there being no perceivable cause and effect, and so the only way to function in this domain is to take quick action to stabilize a situation and attempt to move back into one of the other domains (simple, complicated, or complex) (Table 7.2). WASH in a humanitarian crisis context (such as a cholera outbreak) is an example of a situation that could be defined as chaotic, as is WASH in a natural disaster situation (e.g. a typhoon or flood). In these contexts, rapid communication channels such as those provided through humanitarian emergency response communications via social media and the traditional media may be prioritized. The humanitarian disaster response sector has developed mechanisms to share information quickly, to help stabilize the situations they are facing. These include the UN cluster mechanism introduced in 2005 which supports clear responsibilities for coordination, the strengthening of system-wide preparedness, contingency planning, and technical response capacity. The UN cluster mechanism improves predictability and accountability in chaotic situations (IASC, 2015).

WASH, learning, and the 12 leverage points

Besides understanding a situation according to the Cynefin framework, it is also important to consider where it is best to intervene to maximize positive change in a situation (Abson et al., 2017; Meadows, 1999). Sustainability scholars have found that many sustainability interventions have targeted tangible, short-term interventions that are easier to implement, but that these interventions have limited potential for bringing about transformational change (Abson et al., 2017). The high failure rate of WASH infrastructure (UNDP Water Governance Facility/UNICEF, 2015) could be considered an example of this. To assist the process of deciding where to intervene in a system, Meadows (1999) developed the '12 leverage points framework'. Leverage points in this context are specific feedback processes or activities in a system where a small change could lead to an eventual overall change in the system's behaviour (Meadows, 1999).

According to Meadows (2002), to stay a learner requires us to have the courage to make mistakes and to be able to admit to not knowing. In this vulnerable state, 'the way you learn is by experiment[ing] … by trial and error' (Meadows, 2002: 5). She argues that learning happens through taking 'small steps, constant monitoring, and a willingness to change course as you find out more about where it's leading' (Meadows, 2002: 5). Learning, in this sense, is an adaptive approach to the emergent behaviour (Table 7.1) of the systems and situations that an organization is working within. This is important for the WASH sector, because the ways in which problems are framed and knowledge is produced influence policy development and societal outcomes (Abson et al., 2017). Other authors from the field of transformative sustainability also believe that learning processes that take account of complexity, uncertainty, and management of the commons emerge from 'open and iterative cycles of experimentation, observation, analysis, and judgement of results' (König, 2018: 15). In line with Freire's (1970) treatise on two-way education, this allows for solutions to sustainability issues to emerge from the process of shared learning.

Table 7.3 Twelve leverage points put forward by Meadows in 1999 mapped against examples from the WASH sector

Leverage points (Meadows, 1999)	Examples of situations from the WASH sector	Types of WASH learning approaches that work well with this leverage level
The table begins with leverage point 12, which is the one that is least effective for leveraging, and ends with leverage point 1, the most effective point.		
12. Constants, parameters, numbers (such as subsidies, taxes, and standards)	• Water quality targets • Standards for building toilets and septic schemes	Learning processes that facilitate the exchange of technical information and the development of appropriate norms around targets, safety standards, and design of WASH-related infrastructure
11. The sizes of buffers and other stabilizing stocks, relative to their flows	• Capacity of water reservoirs • Capacity of wastewater treatment plants	
10. The structure of material stocks and flows (such as transport networks, population age structures)	• Well-designed sewerage networks and community-based sanitation schemes • Well-designed piped water schemes • Fixing poorly designed water and sanitation infrastructure	
9. The lengths of delays, relative to the rate of system change	• Managing groundwater pollution from human waste • Water scarcity induced by over-use or climate change	Learning processes that facilitate and draw on feedback loops, respond to monitoring and evaluation, and develop systematized learning from this monitoring and evaluation and experience
8. The strength of negative feedback loops, relative to the impacts they are trying to correct	• Compliance for faecal sludge management (safe storage, transport, treatment, and disposal) • Managing waterborne diseases caused by poor WASH	
7. The gain around driving positive feedback loops	• Cost-benefit analysis of WASH demonstrating that the benefits to society outweigh the costs of WASH (see Hutton, 2015) • Incentives for communities to transition to open defecation-free status	

(continues)

Table 7.3 (*continued*)

Leverage points (Meadows, 1999)	Examples of situations from the WASH sector	Types of WASH learning approaches that work well with this leverage level
6. The structure of information flows (who does and does not have access to information)	• Real-time information about water consumption leading to changes in water use behaviours • Water pricing which responds to different customer types, uses, and amounts of water available • Community identification of who does and does not have a latrine in a community	Learning processes that address who does and does not have access to information, and facilitate inclusive and participatory learning opportunities. The power dynamics around knowledge and learning are considered and addressed.
5. The rules of the system (such as incentives, punishments, constraints)	• States being duty bound to ensure all their citizens have the Human Right to Water and Sanitation • Local governments being legally responsible and therefore accountable for water and/or sanitation services • Financial incentives for putting in place or optimally operating WASH infrastructure (at the household level, or national government funding for local government action) • Enforcement strategies for safe faecal sludge management and disposal	
4. The power to add, change, evolve, or self-organize system structure	• Decentralized and diverse WASH strategies that address nexus issues such as energy consumption, pollution, resource use, inequality, and climate change • Locally driven integrated water resources management	

(*continues*)

Table 7.3 (*continued*)

Leverage points (Meadows, 1999)	Examples of situations from the WASH sector	Types of WASH learning approaches that work well with this leverage level
3. The goals of the system	• The Human Rights to Water and Sanitation • The Sustainable Development Goals – Goal 6 in particular • National and local goals and targets	Deep, participatory, egalitarian, and iterative learning processes are core to changing the goals of the system, as is drawing on multiple disciplines through transdisciplinarity. Critical thinking is prioritized, and transformational learning processes are adopted that engage key stakeholders in a change process. Through praxis (the meeting of reflection and action), individuals gain a sense of their own agency, and they can participate in changing the paradigm or mindset of the system. Power relationships between 'teachers' and 'students' are equitable (Freire, 1970), allowing all actors to learn from each other.
2. The mindset or paradigm out of which the system – its goals, structure, rules, delays, parameters – arises	• Gender equality and inclusion in WASH (reducing inequalities) • WASH advocacy campaigns • Strengths-based approaches to WASH • Public/private ownership and responsibility for WASH • Upholding the state's responsibility for ensuring its citizens' Human Rights to Water and Sanitation are recognized and achieved • 'Remunicipalization' (returning water systems from private to public ownership and management structures) • Circular economy informed sanitation strategies	
1. The power to transcend paradigms	• Non-attachment to WASH solutions associated with particular paradigms and ability to see beyond paradigms • Transformative learning through project implementation • 'Critical reflexivity', which enables us to think more critically about our own assumptions and actions, can help us develop more collaborative, responsive, and ethical ways of managing organizations (Cunliffe, 2004: 407).	

The WASH sector is continuously looking for opportunities to create step changes in the sustainability of water and sanitation services and hygiene behaviours. The sector is also increasingly conscious of the inequalities and power relations within societies, which are often inadvertently expressed within WASH programmes. Many WASH issues require more than just engineering and policy responses. The question of who receives sustainable and safely managed WASH services, and who goes without, is often determined by underlying power dynamics, and those dynamics are a manifestation of the prevailing political economy and culture of a society. According to Meadows' leverage points, if interventions are focused at the 'paradigm level', as opposed to the 'standards or technical levels', they are likely to bring about more impactful change (Table 7.3) (Meadows, 1999). At the same time, it is important for the WASH sector to work across the full spectrum of types of interventions: from addressing the 'parameters' of a system (for example the hardware needed for WASH and engineering standards – the 12th leverage point), through to challenging paradigms (the underpinning values, goals, and worldviews of actors that shape how WASH is considered and delivered – the first leverage point).

Decisions related to WASH (and their outcomes) are heavily influenced by macroeconomic and political factors, including taxation (for essential services), principles of user pays and cost recovery (for water and sanitation services), public–private partnerships, human rights (the human rights to water and sanitation), and social safety nets. These factors have influenced the types and sources of knowledge available to the sector, and whose knowledge is legitimized and drawn upon. They have, in turn, influenced decision-making related to WASH at the community, state, and global levels. Paradigms are influenced by dominant cultures and discourses. For example, historically the 'technocratic' paradigms for WASH interventions were found to be inadequate for creating change in the system, and so other paradigms (such as those around the human rights to water and sanitation and gender equality and inclusion) emerged, but they continue to be marginalized as discourses due to the power of dominant paradigms.

The leverage-points framework encourages decision-makers and stakeholders to consider these broader paradigmatic factors, as well as the (lower level) constants, parameters, and numbers when deciding where to intervene in a WASH situation to create positive societal change.

Conclusion

While many WASH organizations have increasingly employed knowledge capture and learning strategies, such strategies have rarely been designed with the use of systems thinking tools. By drawing on the two systems thinking tools canvassed in this chapter, namely the Cynefin framework and Meadows' leverage points, and by using these tools in our processes from the outset, we can make decisions about where to place scarce resources for knowledge and learning more strategically in order to increase leverage. Learning is a key driver of sustainability transformation, but only if inequitable power dynamics are challenged, critical thinking is employed, and learning is truly shared and applied to real-world problems.

In this chapter we have shown that for WASH organizations, choosing the learning processes and tools that are best suited to a particular context depends on the situation they are operating within, and the leverage points that they are working to utilize. WASH organizations are often working in the complicated domain, but more often in the complex domain as defined in the Cynefin framework, leading to the need for real-time learning processes, collaboration, and deep participatory processes. Similarly, WASH organizations are often working to utilize leverage points associated with the lower levels of Meadow's leverage points hierarchy (1999), and therefore trialling, experimentation, and feedback loops are important. Beyond this, the larger-scale system-wide changes needed to support equitable and inclusive WASH improvements at scale require the use of the higher levels of Meadows' (1999) hierarchy, and require truly participatory and iterative learning processes that draw on transdisciplinary forms of knowledge.

The importance of the organizational context supporting and driving knowledge and learning processes within and between WASH organizations was also considered in this chapter, since it is in such organizational environments that different learning processes and tools are embedded. Drawing on previous research, we conclude that a critical factor is the role leaders play in providing space and support for staff to learn and apply monitoring and evaluation processes (feedback loops) (Grant et al., 2016). Deakin Crick's (2012) conception of learning journeys, and Freire's (1970) focus on dialogue, action, and critical reflection, support the need for organizations to provide learning environments in which people can learn within their jobs, drawing on the appropriate knowledge and learning processes and tools (that match the situation and the intervention), and experimenting with these in an adaptive manner.

In conclusion, we suggest that systems thinking concepts such as those described in this chapter can provide WASH practitioners with tools and ways of thinking that can help them to:

- better understand the situation that they are working within, and how this may influence the types of learning tools and processes that would be appropriate to use in that domain;
- make informed judgements about where in a system to direct attention and activity in order to maximize leverage and drive sustainable change processes and orient learning processes to complement the chosen leverage point;
- choose from among the options for building knowledge and learning processes into WASH interventions, recognizing that understanding how knowledge flows through a system, including inequities in access to knowledge, is a key leverage point in itself.

Responses to the Sustainable Development Goals call for systems thinking approaches, given the interrelated nature of the Goals. The systems thinking tools presented in this chapter are useful for supporting such approaches, and could be incorporated into existing and well-established processes used by the global WASH sector, such as designing theories of change, developing knowledge and learning plans and communications strategies, and delivering on the learning component of monitoring, evaluation, and learning. With deeper and more strategic thinking, the WASH sector could offer a great deal to the application of systems thinking, and could better support adaptive WASH interventions and associated knowledge and learning processes and products.

Acknowledgements

The authors are indebted to the ideas and contributions provided by Isabel Sebastian, Federico Davila Cisneros, and Cynthia Mitchell in the development of this chapter.

References

Abson, D.J., Fischer, J., Leventon, J., Newig, J., Schomerus, T., Vilsmaier, U., von Wehrden, H., Abernethy, P., Ives, C.D., Jager, N.W., and Lang, D.J. (2017) 'Leverage points for sustainability transformation', *Ambio* 46(1): 30–9 <https://doi.org/10.1007/s13280-016-0800-y>.

Arnold, R.D. and Wade, J.P. (2015) 'A definition of systems thinking: a systems approach', *Procedia Computer Science* 44: 669–78 <https://doi.org/10.1016/j.procs.2015.03.050>.

Centre for Affordable Water and Sanitation Technology (CAWST) (2014) *Latrine Design and Construction Workshop* [online], December 2014 <https://resources.cawst.org/agenda/0c6da648/latrine-design-and-construction-5-day-workshop-agenda-for-participants> [accessed 15 April 2018].

Checkland, P. (2000) 'Soft systems methodology: a thirty year retrospective', *Systems Research and Behavioral Science* 17: S11–S58 <https://doi.org/10.1002/1099-1743(200011)17:1+<::AID-SRES374>3.0.CO;2-O>.

Cunliffe, A.L. (2004) 'On becoming a critically reflexive practitioner', *Journal of Management Education* 28(4): 407–26 <https://doi.org/10.1177/1052562904264440>.

da Silva-Wells, C. and Verhoeven, J. (2013) *Resource Centre Networks: Contributing to a Learning and Adaptive WASH Sector* [pdf], The Hague, Netherlands: IRC <https://www.ircwash.org/sites/default/files/rcns_contributng_to_sector_learning_2009-2012.pdf> [accessed 10 March 2018].

Deakin Crick, R. (2012) 'Deep engagement as a complex system: identity, learning power and authentic enquiry', in S. Christenson, A. Reschly, and C. Wylie (eds), *Handbook of Research on Student Engagement,* Boston, MA: Springer.

Deakin Crick, R., Haigney, D., Huang, S., Coburn, T., and Goldspink, C. (2012) 'Learning power in the workplace: the effective lifelong learning inventory and its reliability and validity and implications for learning and development', *The International Journal of Human Resource Management* 24(11): 2255–72 <https://doi.org/10.1080/09585192.2012.725075>.

Freire, P. (1970) *Pedagogy of the Oppressed,* New York, NY: Herder and Herder.

Grant, M., Murta, J., Willetts, J., and Carrard, N. (2016) *Civil Society Organizations' Learning for Impact in Water, Sanitation and Hygiene Programming* [online], CS WASH Fund <www.cswashfund.org/shared-resources/references/report-csos-learning-impact-wash> [accessed 1 September 2017].

Holling, C.S. (1978) *Adaptive Environmental Assessment and Management,* London: John Wiley.

Hutton, G. (2015) *Benefits and Costs of the Water Sanitation and Hygiene Targets for the Post-2015 Development Agenda. Post-2015 Consensus,* Tewksbury, MA: Copenhagen Consensus Centre.

Inter-Agency Standing Committee (IASC) (2015) *IASC Reference Module for Cluster Coordination at the Country Level* [online] <https://www.humanitarianresponse.info/en/coordination/clusters/document/iasc-reference-module-cluster-coordination-country-level-0> [accessed 24 April 2018].

ISF-UTS and SNV (2016) *Are We Doing the Right Thing? Critical Questioning for City Sanitation Planning,* prepared by Institute for Sustainable Futures, University of Technology Sydney and SNV Netherlands Development Organization.

Ison, R. (2008) 'Systems thinking and practice for action research', in P. Reason and H. Bradbury (eds), *The Sage Handbook of Action Research Participative Inquiry and Practice* (2nd edn), pp. 139–58, London: Sage Publications.

König, A. (2018) 'Sustainability science as a transformative social learning process', in A. König and J. Ravetz (eds), *Sustainability Science: Key Issues,* London: Earthscan/Routledge.

Meadows, D. (1997) 'Places to intervene in a system', *Whole Earth,* Winter 1997 [pdf] <https://www.conservationgateway.org/ConservationPlanning/cbd/guidance-document/key-advances/Documents/Meadows_Places_to_Intervene.pdf> [accessed 20 April 2018].

Meadows, D. (1999) *Leverage Points: Places to Intervene in a System,* Hartland, VT: The Sustainability Institute.

Meadows, D. (2002) 'Dancing with systems', *The Systems Thinker* 13(2): 2–6 [online] <https://thesystemsthinker.com/dancing-with-systems/> [accessed 24 April 2018].

Meadows, D. (2008) *Thinking in Systems: A Primer,* White River Junction, VT: Chelsea Green Publishing.

Open University (2005) 'Systems thinking: a select glossary' [online] <www.open.edu/openlearn/money-management/management/leadership-and-management/managing/systems-thinking-select-glossary> [accessed 26 April 2018].

Padilla, A. and Dumpert, J. (2017) *'The influence of real time learning in WASH programming',* Paper 2681, Proceedings of the 40th WEDC International Conference, Loughborough, UK.

Senge, P. (1990, revised 2006) *The Fifth Discipline: The Art and Practice of the Learning Organization,* New York, NY: Doubleday.

Snowden, D. (2002) 'Complex acts of knowing: paradox and descriptive self-awareness', *Journal of Knowledge Management* 6(2): 100–11 <https://doi.org/10.1108/13673270210424639>.

Snowden, D. (2005) 'Strategy in the context of uncertainty', *Handbook of Business Strategy* 6(1): 47–54 <https://doi.org/10.1108/08944310510556955>.

Snowden, D. and Boone, M. (2007) 'A leader's framework for decision making', *Harvard Business Review* 85(11): 68–76.

Stafford-Smith, M., Griggs, D., Gaffney, O., Ullah, F., Reyers, B., Kanie, N., Stigson, B., Shrivastava, P., Leach, M., and O'Connell, D. (2016) 'Integration: the key to implementing the Sustainable Development Goals', *Sustainability Science* 12(6): 911–9 <https://doi.org/10.1007/s11625-016-0383-3>.

Taylor, D.L., Kahawita, T.M., Cairncross, S., and Ensink, J.H.J. (2015) 'The impact of water, sanitation and hygiene interventions to control cholera: a systematic review', *PLoS ONE* 10(8): 1–19 <https://doi.org/10.1371/journal.pone.0135676>.

Tilley, E., Strande, L., Lüthi, C., Mosler, H-J., Udert, K.M., Gebauer, H., and Hering, J. (2014) 'Looking beyond technology: an integrated approach to water, sanitation and hygiene in low income countries', *Environmental Science and Technology* 48(17): 9965–70 <https://doi.org/10.1021/es501645d>.

Ulrich, W. and Reynolds, M. (2010) 'Critical systems heuristics', in M. Reynolds and S. Holwell (eds), *Systems Approaches to Managing Change: A Practical Guide*, pp. 243–92, London: Springer.

UNDP Water Governance Facility/UNICEF (2015) *Accountability in WASH: Explaining the Concept* [pdf], Accountability for Sustainability Partnership, Stockholm: UNDP Water Governance Facility at SIWI; New York: UNICEF <https://www.unicef.org/wash/files/Accountability_in_WASH_Explaining_the_Concept.pdf> [accessed 20 April 2018].

UNICEF (2014) 'UNICEF Sanitation Marketing Series' [online] <https://www.unicef.org/wash/3942_documents.html> [accessed 20 March 2018].

Visscher, J.T., Pels, J., Markowski, V., and De Graaf, S. (2006) *Knowledge and Information Management in the Water and Sanitation Sector: A Hard Nut to Crack*, Thematic Overview Paper 14, June 2006, The Hague, Netherlands: IRC International Water and Sanitation Centre.

Whatley, B. (2013) 'Improved learning for greater effectiveness in development NGOs', *Development in Practice* 23(8): 963–76 <https://doi.org/10.1080/09614524.2013.840563>.

WHO and UNICEF (2015) *Water, Sanitation and Hygiene in Health Care Facilities: Status in Low- and Middle-Income Countries and Way Forward* [online] <www.who.int/water_sanitation_health/publications/wash-health-care-facilities/en/> [accessed 28 April 2018].

Wickson, F., Carew, A.L., and Russell, A.W. (2006) 'Transdisciplinary research: characteristics, quandaries and quality', *Futures* 38(9): 1046–59 <https://doi.org/10.1016/j.futures.2006.02.011>.

About the authors

Melita Grant is a practitioner, adviser, and researcher in integrated water resources management (IWRM) and water, sanitation, and hygiene (WASH), with a focus on gender equality and inclusion. Melita has worked in state and local government, universities, and civil society organizations (CSOs). With an academic background in Political Science and Environmental Management,

Melita has specialized in transdisciplinary approaches to addressing sustainability challenges. Melita has led a range of projects focused on gender equality within WASH and IWRM for international donors, CSOs, and global partnerships. She authored the Global Water Partnership 'Action Piece' on gender equality and water resources management, which was adopted by the United Nations High Level Panel on Water in 2018.

Professor Juliet Willetts, University of Technology, Sydney, is a researcher, adviser, and evaluator in the field of international development aid. A recognized leader informing WASH policy and practice in the Asia and Pacific region, Juliet has led four major research grants, undertaken more than 50 research projects, and has been presented with several research excellence and leadership awards. Juliet's work is transdisciplinary, spanning socio-cultural, institutional, economic, and technical dimensions, and involves collaboration with donors, partner governments, and non-governmental agencies. She is a founding member of the Australian Water, Sanitation and Hygiene Reference group, a policy reference group and community of practice that leads efforts to improve effectiveness of WASH interventions in the region.

CHAPTER 8

Measuring impact in WASH from a complex adaptive systems perspective

Chris Brown

Abstract

Contemporary approaches to monitoring and evaluation (M&E) rely on using static indicators to assess a system that is fundamentally in flux. This chapter will look at the challenges of current approaches and provide insights into how to restructure the way we measure our impact on whole systems, rather than just individual processes. This chapter will explain how to adopt a system view of your operating environment, how to map that system to understand its interconnectedness and inherent complexity, and then how to identify the true drivers of the system to allow for the creation of a range of metrics that measure the health of the system rather than just the level of its outputs. This process will include identifying the key factors that form the foundation for a functioning system, and the concept of viewing a system through a dynamic set of living indicators rather than through the static success indicators used in the sector. Expanding on resilient systems thinking, we will examine how best to use this knowledge to design a monitoring system that produces meaningful insights into the performance of the system as a whole, through a deeper understanding of the enabling environment in which it operates.

Keywords: monitoring and evaluation, complexity, WASH, adaptive M&E

BEING ABLE TO MEASURE AND PROVIDE evidence for impact is one of the fundamental requirements of development interventions to prove the efficacy of their work. To meet this demand, the linear nature of traditional development approaches has created an equally linear set of approaches to the monitoring and evaluation (M&E) of projects and programmes. At the core of this traditional approach lies the logical framework with its array of output indicators against which progress is tracked over time.

The problem with these existing methodologies lies in their reliance on 'comparative static analysis' (Page, 2011), whereby static indicators are used to provide a situational snapshot of the progress made against predefined parameters. While such an approach makes it possible to measure some of the impacts within a system, within a given context, and at a specific moment in time, complex adaptive systems (CAS) are constantly in a state of reactive flux. So although static indicators can provide valuable inductive insights

http://dx.doi.org/10.3362/9781780447483.008

into the momentary mechanics of the system, to fully understand the true function and impact of those mechanics and the vast array of interactions they produce within the system, we need to adopt a more deductive form of reasoning (Haggis, 2010). In essence, by accepting the true complexity of CAS we are acknowledging the need for more complex tools with which to assess them (Pearce and Merletti, 2006). Ultimately, there are no simple or concrete answers; rather, the solutions, like the systems themselves, need to become more complex, interrelated, and dynamic.

In this chapter, this principle is examined in greater detail to try to understand how it might be possible to unpick the complex interconnectedness of a system to identify the key drivers that best measure the true health of the system. This process fits neatly into the Framed Adaptation approach, the principle of which is the creation of a framework within the enabling environment, within which processes can best adapt and evolve to work within the context, skill base, and resource base available (Brown, 2019). However, to do this on a level that gives us sufficient insight into the mechanics of the system, we need to look at both the enabling and operating environment in greater detail.

The simplest way to start this process of unravelling the embedded complexity of systems and their networks is to map the web of interconnections that exist between agents or processes (Bodin et al., 2006; Knoke and Yang, 2008; Scott, 2000; Wasserman and Faust, 1994). To understand a CAS at the agent level, the most popular method is to use Social Network Analysis (SNA) (which has been outlined as an approach in more detail by McNicholl (2019)), while for understanding the drivers and influencers on different variables within a system, a causal loop diagram is useful (see Liddle and Fenner, 2019). For both approaches the principle remains the same: namely, to unpack the mess of interconnected relationships between nodes to produce an objective map of the network interactions and to understand the mechanics of what drives them. This is particularly helpful in developing a system view of the operating environment because it helps to clarify the direction of relationships (i.e. the direction in which processes generally flow between agents), identify important hubs (agents that have a high degree of connections with other agents), as well as increase our understanding of the ease with which connections are made and broken and the robustness of the network as a whole.

It is helpful to explain here how this process can be useful for unpacking the types of indicators that should be used for monitoring the health of CAS. Limiters and adaptive behaviours can be shaped at an enabling- and operating-environment level to help influence the behaviour of agents within the system and therefore influence the potential emergent behaviour of the system as a whole. In a CAS, the operating environment that we want to measure is in a state of constant adaptive flux and these outcome-influencing limiters and adaptive behaviours operate in a state of constant counteraction. The limiters can therefore be used almost like a gyroscope to constantly assess the level and direction of adaptation to their influence, and then be adapted to help coerce the system back into the state of dynamic equilibrium that best suits the direction of adaptation that the intervention is trying to achieve.

These limiters and adaptive behaviours can then be used as benchmarking indicators for the overall health of the system, telling us whether the system is adapting in a way that is producing reinforcing or balancing feedback loops. Reinforcing feedback loops drive change either towards growth or dissolution (i.e. potential emergent behaviour), while balancing feedback loops work to maintain homeostasis within the system. If we apply a plant analogy to explain the principle of growing a system, this is like measuring indicators such as soil pH, water content, and access to sunlight to determine how likely a plant is to grow or bear fruit, rather than simply measuring the height of a plant, or how much fruit it is bearing at a given point in time. This may sound fairly simplistic, but it gives us a much clearer insight into the extent to which each driver is influencing the way that the plant is behaving, allowing us to monitor the system more closely and adapt more quickly to changes as they occur.

By measuring the health of the system, rather than the static status of its components at a given time, we are getting a much clearer insight into how likely a system is to evolve along the desired trajectory. This allows us to adjust the limiters to help the system adapt in a constructive way, while also giving us invaluable insight into the mechanics of the system, and into how the system we have mapped is actually behaving. This is one of the fundamental principles of adaptive programming. Being able to benchmark the process and track the overall health of the system against those benchmarks is key to being able to react and respond to system behaviours, by triggering the appropriate feedback loops that may then trigger emergent behaviour within the system. Figure 8.1 outlines a process flow diagram of how this approach can be structured.

If we understand and accept this approach, then we open ourselves up to a whole new set of challenges: namely, to attempt to map out the complexity of the system and draw out a set of living indicators that will best reflect the ongoing health of the system.

Starting with the network mapping process, I would like to propose a slight variation to the normal approach to SNA. The most important thing with network analysis is to get good data into the process, so that you can draw more meaningful analysis out. The problem with using SNA in isolation is that while it helps us *see* the system in a more holistic way, it does not directly help us to *understand* the behaviour of the system. So we need to use both SNA and causal loop diagrams as tools to help us apply CAS thinking to the mapping of process interactions within the system. When we do this in combination, we end up with a network landscape that highlights nodes of strong connectivity and potential influence, and nodes that are lacking sufficient connectivity to exercise the various processes that lie under their remit.

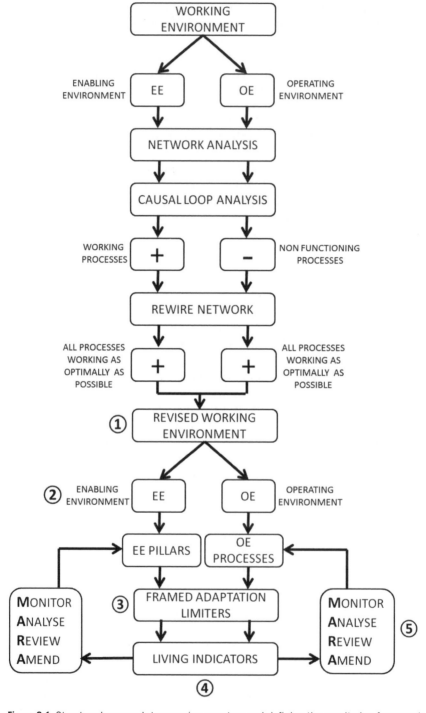

Figure 8.1 Structured approach to mapping a system and defining the monitoring framework

We can now apply the above process to a case study of the rural water sector in Tanzania. The case study is described in more detail by Brown (2019) in Chapter 6 of this book. When the network of interrelations was mapped between the primary stakeholders involved in rural water supply at the start of the programme (Figure 8.2), it was clearly evident that the District Water Engineer (DWE) was the central hub of the network with relatively little support from other nodes in the network.

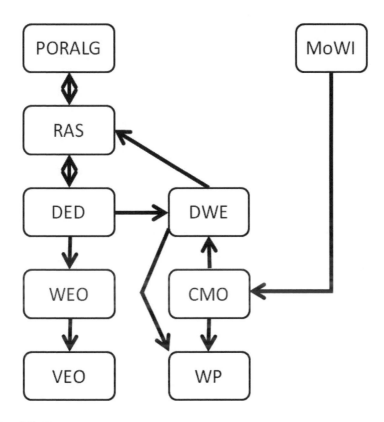

Abbreviations

CMO	community management organization
DED	district executive director
DWE	district water engineer
MoWI	Ministry of Water and Irrigation
PORALG	President's Office for Regional and Local Government
RAS	regional administrative secretary
VEO	village executive officer
WEO	ward executive officer
WP	water point

Figure 8.2 Basic SNA structure of operational relationships in Tanzania rural water sector

However, when the planned process flow was mapped in an influence diagram at an operational level, as shown in Figure 8.3, it became clear that, in the way the process framework was structured, the DWEs and community management organizations (CMOs) should have a far more complex and interconnected relationship. When this process was reviewed, it became clear that the lack of these connections in the real-world network was placing an enormous burden on the DWE, producing demands that they often did not have the time, resources, or capacity to meet, and this was in turn having a very negative impact on both the quality of water point data and on the ability of DWEs to use this data for effective operations and maintenance (O&M).

To address this it was necessary to look back at the influencing pillars to understand which pillars needed to be focused on to instigate the desired adaptive changes in the network, which would in turn allow the system to function in a structure that is much closer to the optimum, from an operational environment perspective.

By focusing on engaging political will to address the systemic issues in the rural water sector, it allowed the Ministry of Water and Irrigation (MoWI) to properly engage the President's Office Regional Administration and Local Government (PORALG) to collectively commit to strengthening accountability from the local government side (Regional Administrative Secretary (RAS), District Water Engineer (DWE), District Executive Director (DED), Ward

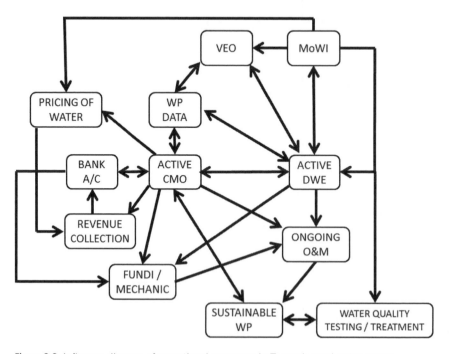

Figure 8.3 Influence diagram of operational processes in Tanzania rural water sector

Executive Officer (WEO), Village Executive Officer (VEO)), which in turn helped influence the improvement in the timely reporting of data through local government structures. This provided a window of opportunity for MoWI to adapt and improve its community management approach to engaging and registering CMOs and community owned water supply organizations (COWSOs). The Central Data Management Team (CDMT) could then align the CMO with the VEO at village level, to create a data submission process that was assured of timely reporting by the local government side (VEO), and assured of integrity of data by the community side (CMO), thereby maintaining the improvement in data reporting, while guarding against the misreporting or gaming of data. The adaptive by-product of this increased interconnectedness, as seen in Figure 8.4, is a mutually agreed cooperation that leads to increased accountability as both parties at village level become, in effect, self-policing agents to one another.

Referring back to Figure 8.1, once the working environment ① had been restructured to better reflect the intended operating environment on the ground, it was possible to review the enabling and operating environment pillars and processes ②, to ensure that they aligned with the relationships within the working environment and that they were implementable under this structure. Once these processes were in place, it was relatively straightforward to establish a set of framed adaptation limiters for the system ③. The framed adaptation limiters for the system were embedded at various levels within the enabling and operating environments. Limiters focused largely on influencing the levels of transparency and accountability in the system, as key drivers of operational efficiency and as positive feedback influencers on political engagement and data improvement. The primary list of limiters included:

- data updating methodology requirements – timing, format, and content;
- data quality key performance indicators (KPIs) – completeness and correctness threshold requirements for data;
- adaptive performance payment structures;
- COWSO registration requirements;
- COWSO reporting requirements;
- local government accountability structure (PORALG – RAS – DWE – WEO – VEO); and
- rehabilitation requirements, rates, and reporting.

The limiters act as structural and operational guidelines, designed to influence the likelihood that relevant agents behave in a constructive system-enforcing way (i.e. agents are encouraged to operate within the guidelines of the limiters, and in doing so are more likely to produce desired behaviour for the system). Therefore we need to monitor and track both the behaviour of the agent *and* the effectiveness of the limiter (i.e. the restrictiveness of the limiter and the ease with which the agent can perform the process). There is a 'Goldilocks' principle here, whereby we don't want the limiter to be *too controlling,* thereby restricting the ability of the agents to fulfil their roles or adapt their processes over time. Equally, we don't want the limiter to be *too*

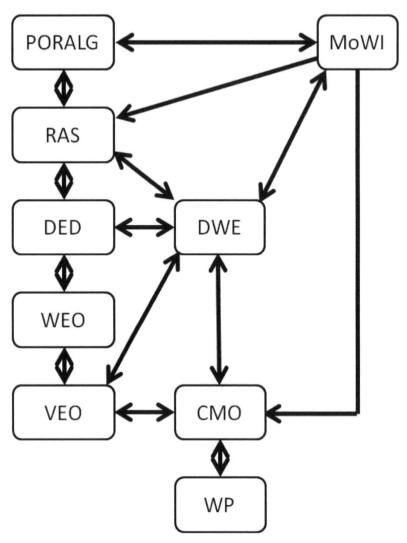

Abbreviations

CMO   community management organization
DED   district executive director
DWE   district water engineer
MoWI   Ministry of Water and Irrigation
PORALG   President's Office for Regional and Local Government
RAS   regional administrative secretary
VEO   village executive officer
WEO   ward executive officer
WP   water point

Figure 8.4 Revised SNA structure of operational relationships in Tanzania rural water sector (note the changes compared with Figure 8.2)

weak, allowing the agent to not fulfil their role to the requisite level, thereby damaging the overall process and the efficacy of the system as a whole.

Once the limiters are defined, we can work on drawing up a list of indicators for monitoring ④. As has been discussed earlier in the chapter, the aim here is to design a list of living indicators that can best track the health of the system. These need to be based around the structures and processes that are necessary for the system to succeed. To do this we need to combine both *input* indicators (i.e. indicators from the enabling environment, operating environment, and limiter list that define and influence how the system evolves) and *output* indicators (i.e. static comparative indicators that measure outputs or performance of the system at a specific point in time). This is a redefining of the standard input and output logframe definitions that seeks to distinguish between indicators that contribute to behaviour change, and those that simply measure it.

This probably still seems quite conceptual to you at this point, so let me share some examples of the types of indicators that might be considered at each level of the process, using the Tanzania context that we have been discussing. Table 8.1 lists some examples of the types of potential indicators

Table 8.1 Example input and output indicators for the enabling environment of the rural water sector in Tanzania

Aim	Indicator	Definition	Type
MoWI – PORALG political engagement	Management support, attendance at strategy meetings, commitment to problem resolution	Quarterly meetings attendance, payment by results (PbR) focal person's action points met	Input
Water point data improvement	MoWI commitment to data quality improvement and alignment of results framework	Water quality treatment and testing plan design and implementation	Input
	MoWI commitment to M&E framework and sustainability framework	Frameworks implemented across all sections of Rural Water Supply Directorate (RWSD)	Input
Local government accountability	RAS engagement in DWE updating process and O&M improvements	RAS engagement with CDMT, DWE performance records	Input
Financial model to incentivize and drive water point sustainability	Payment structure adapted to Local Government Authority (LGA) reporting frequency, data quality, and O&M	Data accuracy and reporting records/payment disbursement tracking by LGA	Input/ output

Table 8.2 Example output indicators for the operating environment of the rural water sector in Tanzania

Aim	Indicator	Definition	Type
CDMT management	CDMT adequately funded and equipped and performance reviewed	Quarterly CDMT process and management performance review	Output
Improved community management	New COWSO registration process implemented and tracked	Agreed COWSO registration targets tracked monthly	Output
Improved O&M	O&M indicator added to DWE/COWSO monthly reporting requirements	Submission of O&M data tracked through DWE monthly update report	Output
Data reporting	Monthly inventory update report to be submitted by all DWEs each month	LGA reporting frequency and quality tracked and reported to RAS	Output
Data quality	Data quality assessed monthly and annually through completeness and accuracy of data	Monthly field- and phone-level spot checks by CDMT and external verifiers	Output
Shift to service level approach	Service level indicators phased in over agreed timeline	Indicators added to monthly update and tracked	Output
RWSD capacity building	Embedded technical advisory support to CDMT and management provided for ongoing capacity building	Technical Advisor impact assessment and process and performance review	Output
LG engagement and accountability	PORALG and local government (RAS and DWE) adherence to agreed actions	Quarterly management review of performance of local government	Output

drawn from the enabling environment. Table 8.2 lists some examples of the types of potential indicators drawn from the operating environment in the Tanzanian example. Table 8.3 shows the selection of indicators that can be adapted from these to create the limiters in the Tanzanian example.

The resulting framework of indicators provides us with a means by which to monitor the key inputs at the enabling environment level, track the more standardized process indicators at the operational level, and then review and

Table 8.3 Example of indicators used to create limiters for adaptation in the rural water sector in Tanzania

Aim	Triggers for adaptation	Elements to adapt
Data updating methodology requirements – timing, format, and content	• LGA reporting performance • Failure to meet update deadline • Data submitted in wrong format • DWE feedback on methodology	• DWE reporting burden • Simplicity of updating mechanism • Communication of methodology
Data quality KPIs – completeness and correctness threshold requirements for data	• Monthly update completeness • CDMT internal verification analysis • External verification results	• Data completeness and correctness qualification thresholds • Qualification criteria for PbR
Adaptive performance payment structures	• LGA performance levels • Data quality improvement levels • Operational results framework	• Payment thresholds for PbR • Structure and timings of payments • Strictness of qualification criteria
COWSO registration requirements	• Missing COWSO registration KPI • Lack of transition of CMOs/COWSO • Poor COWSO performance	• Number of criteria for registration • Level of MoWI technical support • Level of COWSO independence • Transition process from the village water committee • PORALG/DWE/RAS engagement
COWSO reporting requirements	• Quality of O&M • Levels of existing reporting • Financial data management and reporting • Efficacy of COWSO operational structure	• Level of direct COWSO support • Complexity of O&M indicators • Number of O&M indicators • Restrictions/constraints on COWSO operational structure

(*continues*)

Table 8.3 (*continued*)

Aim	Triggers for adaptation	Elements to adapt
Local government accountability structure (PORALG – RAS – DWE – WEO – VEO)	• DWE reporting performance • Data accuracy improvement • COWSO/VEO engagement	• MoWI – PORALG engagement of political commitment • Performance related disbursement • COWSO engagement plan and related targets
Rehabilitation requirements, rates, and reporting	• Reported levels of rehabilitation • Average cost of rehabilitation (by infrastructure type) • Functional coverage	• Rehabilitation remuneration structure • Rehabilitation assignment of responsibilities (CMO-DWE) • Spare parts and mechanic-support framework

analyse the data from these indicator sets to understand the trajectory of the system and the origins of the behaviour driving that trajectory. These insights can then be used to reassess the limiters, which can then be readjusted to produce a series of counteracting influences on the system that will help to realign agent behaviour in a way that will nurture constructive outcomes across the broader system. This process can be used in conjunction with conventional M&E approaches, allowing actors to continue to track progress against static operating output indicators while using the enabling environment input indicators to help understand the reasons for observed behaviour and to adapt the system to produce better outcomes. What is important is the ability to differentiate between the observable operational performance and the wider (often more obscure) system mechanics. Actors are increasingly collecting data at the operational level. This gives a very detailed picture of what is happening at a specific point in time but gives no real insight into why. By collecting a broader spectrum of indicators across both the enabling and operating environments, we can start to develop an understanding of the network of interactions in the system and the behavioural drivers that define them.

In reviewing this list of indicators, you may have noticed that many of the actual data collection indicators are in fact comparative static indicators (CSIs) (i.e. a static snapshot of a situation at a specific point in time). This will no doubt prompt the question as to why we are using CSIs having so heavily criticized them as being inappropriate for monitoring a dynamic system.

The answer is a simple one – for most activities we are tied to CSIs as the only means of obtaining a timely, consistent measure that is referenceable. The issue is not specifically with the indicator, but with the way it is used, and in the value and credence that is placed upon it. If you review most logical and M&E frameworks, the indicator list usually makes a lot of sense. However, very often the way these indicators and the data they produce are interpreted, does not. The principal issue here is that many of these indicators are quite linear in their nature, and as such do not tell us much about the true mechanics of the system because they are just a single thread in a very complex web of interactions. If, however, we can acknowledge that this complexity inherently exists and is a natural characteristic of these types of social system, then we can start to weave together some of these threads to create a more informative picture of how the hidden mechanics of these types of systems are really operating.

The key to this is to be constantly reviewing the data ⑤ received back from the monitoring of the process indicators (from both the enabling and operating environment) from the context of the overall system behaviour. This review process should question whether all of the necessary components are in place to help promote adaptive behaviour from within the agent population, by asking questions such as: Is there sufficient cooperation among agents? Are agents happy with the process structure? Is there any gaming going on within the process? And are there signs of adaptive learning?

It must be remembered at this juncture that for adaptive programming to work there must be the space for agents to fail, and then learn from their failure, and that it is likely to take multiple iterations of the process for the agent to learn to adapt. To help expedite this process, phases of iteration should be kept relatively short, for example using monthly updating data to drive an ongoing review process that leads to adaptive changes to the limiters on an ad hoc basis. Each iteration therefore becomes its own cycle of learning and adaptation, from which the individual and collective agent behaviour should improve and evolve. As an approach this takes a more long-term view on change, accepting not only that there will be failures and down trends along the way, but also that there should be a strong commitment throughout to learning from these periods and that over time the net change will be constructive.

By adapting the M&E process to mirror the state of dynamic flux that exists in the operating environment, it allows the intervention to constantly adapt and evolve while still tracking progress and impact along the way. This ceases to be M&E simply for reporting's sake and becomes an integral part of the learning and feedback mechanism that is so essential to an adaptive programme.

References

Bodin, Ö., Crona, B., and Ernstson, H. (2006) 'Social networks in natural resource management: what is there to learn from a structural perspective?' *Ecology and Society* 11(2): r2 <https://dx.doi.org/ 10.2307/26266035>.

Brown, C. (2019) 'Bureaucracy, WASH, and systems thinking', in K. Neely (ed.), *WASH and Systems Thinking*, pp. [page numbers], Rugby: Practical Action Publishing.

Haggis, T. (2010) 'Approaching complexity: a commentary on Keshavarz, Nutbeam, Rowling and Khavarpour', *Social Science and Medicine* 70(10): 1475–7 <http://dx.doi.org/10.1016/j.socscimed.2010.01.022>.

Knoke, D. and Yang, S. (2008) *Social Network Analysis*, Thousand Oaks, CA: Sage Publications Inc.

Liddle, E.S. and Fenner, R.A. (2018) 'Using causal loop diagrams to understand handpump failure in sub-Saharan Africa', in K. Neely (ed.), *WASH and Systems Thinking*, pp. [page numbers], Rugby: Practical Action Publishing.

McNicholl, D. (2018) 'Applying social network analysis to WASH', in K. Neely (ed.), *WASH and Systems Thinking*, pp. [page numbers], Rugby: Practical Action Publishing.

Page, S. (2011) *Diversity and Complexity: Primers in Complex Systems*, Princeton, NJ: Princeton University Press.

Pearce, N. and Merletti, F. (2006) 'Complexity, simplicity, and epidemiology', *International Journal of Epidemiology* 35(3): 515–9 <https://doi.org/10.1093/ije/dyi322>.

Scott, J. (2000) *Social Network Analysis: A Handbook* (2nd edn), Thousand Oaks, CA: Sage Publications Inc.

Wasserman, S. and Faust, K. (1994) *Social Network Analysis: Methods and Applications*, New York: Cambridge University Press.

About the author

Chris Brown is a development consultant specializing in integrated risk management, resilience building, and monitoring and evaluation, with a focus on the WASH sector. He is also the founder and director of WEL Group Consulting. He has an MSc in Environment and Development and over 12 years' experience working on a range of projects for both governments and organizations, including DFID, IRC, the Red Cross Climate Centre, Save the Children, London School of Hygiene and Tropical Medicine, World Vision, and WaterAid. He has extensive experience in the design and implementation of monitoring, evaluation, and mapping processes, particularly in the use of ICT for monitoring and in the design of comprehensive process cycles that incorporate effective and sustainable mechanisms for the collection, analysis, and updating of data inventories. He is also a specialist in the application and integration of complex adaptive systems theory into conventional development approaches to create more sustainable and resilient systems within which development processes can more effectively operate and evolve.

CHAPTER 9

WASH adaptation in Uganda: a practitioner case study

Adam Harvey

Abstract

This chapter looks at a systems approach to WASH management from the perspective of practical activity. It provides a case study of a social enterprise, Whave Solutions, operating currently in Uganda, describing how this non-profit company has taken a dual approach to WASH system analysis and change. As a private-sector service provider, Whave engaged many rural communities in service agreements similar to insurance, pledging to ensure reliable operation of their water sources all year in return for an annual fee. This was attractive to many communities because of frequent and prolonged down-times. Whave's innovation was to pay mechanics monthly for reliable functionality, achieved by training them to follow a preventive maintenance schedule. The other component of the dual approach was to build consensus among stakeholders on desired system outputs, causes of malfunction, and potential solutions suitable for testing. To do this, Whave facilitated workshops with local and central governments, hand-pump mechanics, and NGOs, prompting an ongoing dialogue and leading to public–private partnerships between Whave and local governments. The dialogue has continued intensively since 2013, and the chapter describes how it has generated an iterative approach to system change, with a succession of root problems being addressed: for example, inclusion of politicians, introduction of new legislation, incentivization of local mechanics and community mobilizers, and increasingly detailed structuring of effective public–private partnership procedures.

Keywords: sustainable development, rural water supply, rural WASH, functionality, public–private partnership, preventive maintenance

Successful WASH practice

The desired outputs of a rural WASH system are reduced poverty, better health and education conditions, increased economic security for farmers, a stronger national economy, and conservation of natural resources.

http://dx.doi.org/10.3362/9781780447483.009

A WASH aid practitioner knows the desired WASH result will not be achieved in any community unless certain conditions exist. These conditions are:

- the desired output is clearly defined;
- all factors are taken into account; and
- unwelcome side-effects are guarded against.

Other essential ingredients are knowledge and attention to practical details. Experience in business is valuable, especially knowing what practical constraints and motivations drive actions, which actors have investments and why, and what financial incentives are at play.

Because of the need for all of these conditions to be met, the most effective practitioners often study and work in different sectors, to see how similar problems have been solved. Sector-hopping is a key ingredient of successful practical system analysis and positive innovation.

Conversely, so-called 'high level' thinking does not produce effective system analysis; rather, it is practical thinking and experience on the ground that makes a difference. 'Taking all factors and actors into account' is a precise definition of practical system analysis and effective system change.

In an effort to bring about successful change, Whave, a private-sector service provider, was founded in 2011, in response to indications that aid assistance was not delivering results, with the WASH sector being a clear example. It was registered as Whave Solutions Ltd in Uganda in 2012, with support from central government officials and a remit to work with local government and communities on a comprehensive WASH solution using a results-based finance approach.

Whave's activities in Uganda provide an example and case study of how successful WASH implementation can be brought about using systems analysis integrated with practical activity.

Formulation of a solution

The theory of change is simple, as represented by Figure 9.1.

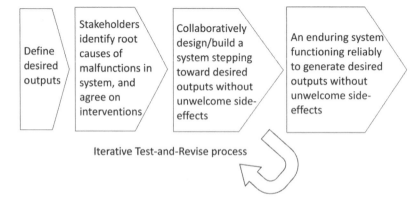

Figure 9.1 Theory of change

Following this theory of change in practice, analysis was conducted collaboratively, with participation of rural communities, local government, central government, local technicians, and a range of stakeholders including Hand Pump Mechanics Associations (HPMAs) and NGOs. This revealed several reasons for failures in WASH service delivery and WASH interventions.

Identifying the problems

Initial identification of malfunctions that frequently prevented success in WASH projects showed:

- Insufficient incentive for technology quality control.
- Low willingness-to-pay tariffs due to (a) poor financial accountability of community leaders, and (b) mistrust between technicians and communities.
- Inadequate rural banking services, although these are needed to build accountability and rural incomes.
- Perverse incentives within community-based maintenance including an absence of minor/major repairs differentiation, no incentive to technicians for preventive maintenance, and Water and Sanitation Committees (WSCs) also making money from repairs.
- Electioneering and patronage culture.
- Inadequate sense of ownership and responsibility for water supply infrastructure.
- Projects are governed by donor needs such as spending a budget within a time period or reaching targets of numbers-of-activities completed or numbers-of-repairs/installations completed rather than by indicators of local economic viability and sustainability. For example if a fixed number of toilets must be installed or a fixed number of hand-pumps rehabilitated by a certain time, the pressure to meet the target is an incentive to over-subsidize and therefore impede local initiative and economic engagement.
- Aid and NGO projects are focused on short-term direct relief instead of long-term institutional strengthening; strategies are designed to suit primary donors, not the system being entered; failure to listen to local system analysts and spokespersons; failure of coordination between aid/NGO organizations and failure to develop common strategy collaboratively with local governments, while paying salaries above local market rates, so weakening local institutions.
- Lack of regulation, lack of clarity as to roles and responsibilities.
- Lack of information about success or failure of hygiene interventions, lack of knowledge of local solutions, lack of interest in hygiene/sanitation solutions, and avoidance of semi-taboo topics.

The identification of malfunctions then leads to an initial design of a functional system.

Suggesting solutions to the problems

The initial design was modified and improved according to the test-and-revise process, which aims to design and build iteratively a functional system, by addressing the root causes identified above, in the following ways:

- For system issues caused by insufficient incentive for technology quality control, and low willingness-to-pay due to mistrust between technicians and communities: introduce the service provider as an organization whose survival depends on technology quality control and which removes financial transaction relationships between local technicians and users.
- For system issues caused by low willingness-to-pay due to poor financial accountability of community leaders, inadequate rural banking services, and WSCs also extracting money from repairs: help establish effective rural banking services, mandate their use by committees, and establish multiple digital supervision of digital bank transaction information to build user confidence in accountability.
- For system issues caused by an absence of minor/major repairs differentiation: structure transactions so that minor and major repairs are both the responsibility of the service utility.
- For system issues caused by lack of incentive to technicians for preventive maintenance: structure services around prevention of breakdowns, with technicians trained in preventive maintenance and paid for reliable functionality, and penalized for breakdowns and prolonged repair.
- For system issues caused by electioneering and patronage culture: establish incentives for politicians to support desired outcomes.
- For system issues caused by inadequate sense of ownership and responsibility for water supply infrastructure and lack of regulation and clarity as to roles and responsibilities: introduce regulations which clarify ownership, roles, and responsibilities.
- For system issues caused by aid and NGO projects focused on short-term direct relief instead of long-term institutional strengthening: develop strategies in each local government area which clearly define what institutional structures are effective and engage local government in clear definitions of roles and responsibilities; build local government capability to actively and effectively regulate partners such as NGOs and private sector actors.
- For system issues caused by aid and NGOs demanding budget spend and number targets: educate donors to understand how these divert from sustainability, establish local government capacity to set viability indicators, monitor, and use the monitoring data to steer aid assistance accordingly.
- For system issues caused by lack of information about success or failure of hygiene interventions, lack of knowledge of local solutions, lack of interest in hygiene/sanitation solutions, and avoidance of semi-taboo

topics: listen to local knowledge and solutions, establish local government capacity for sustained monitoring of success or failure of hygiene interventions, pilot such monitoring, and share information with local authorities.

Assessing the validity of the solutions

Before the solutions are implemented, their feasibility must be realistically assessed.

- The new service utility functions involve cost: monitoring and management of technicians, and technology quality control. Collection of tariffs at cost-recovery levels is difficult in conditions where the sanction of cutting water supply is not available. However, these tariff levels are affordable and acceptable socially, being less than commonly found business rates and the pro-poor tariffs currently proposed by the National Water and Sanitation Corporation of Uganda (NWSC). Collection approaches have to ensure access by all community members, and have to be smart, but both challenges can be met.
- Improved accountability through multiple supervision of bank accounts is feasible.
- Improved WASH regulations which clarify roles and responsibilities are feasible and not difficult to introduce with patience and within a modest capacity-building budget. Their implementation requires a long-term programmatic commitment by funders and aid agencies with some coordination steered by local government, which is feasible.
- Monitoring of effects of hygiene interventions is feasible at affordable sustained costs levels, and sharing of data for analysis and action is feasible.
- Deployment of existing government budget levels to implement improved regulation is feasible.

Addressing issues introduced by initial interventions

- Politicians are numerous, and tend to adopt opposing opinions, so any new regulation promoted by one party is typically opposed by another. This demands fresh strategic thinking.
- Local capacity to regulate coordination of NGO interventions and align them to consistent local government-led long-term strategies is limited, due to the high relative economic power of the NGOs.
- NGO willingness and ability to listen to local government and local spokespersons is very limited.
- Small-scale interventions scattered geographically are not effective in generating social and political consensus for tariff payments and

therefore for a self-sustaining system; saturation of pilot local government areas is essential to create social normalization and act as a pilot from which replication proceeds. However, this implies unequal attention to specific pilot areas, which causes resistance on the grounds of equity. It also can have the effect of pushing a solution onto too small a population rather than creating an economic demand, therefore pilot areas must not be too small geographically.

The process described continues, improving the effectiveness of system change as lessons are learned from practical experience and then applied. The factors described in the list above imply that interventions must not only be carefully designed but must be at a large scale, saturating specific areas.

A case history

2011–2012

In 2011 discussions were held with the Ugandan Ministry of Water and Environment (MWE) proposing the new reliability-oriented incentives for local technicians. Funds were sought with support from the Ministry, and work on detailed programme design started in 2011 and 2012, with personal investment from the Whave founder. This followed a period of three years in which the issue of unreliable rural water supply had been investigated through field visits to rural communities and partnerships with aid organizations.

A major spur behind the founding of Whave was to demonstrate effective sustainable development practice. The failure of aid-funded WASH intervention was plain to see while travelling in rural Uganda. Common observations included unsafe water being collected by families with recently installed handpumps close to their homes but not functioning. There also appeared to be a loss of traditional hygienic practices such as protection of springs through live fencing, use of locally made ladles to transfer water safely from drinking pots, and use of locally grown soft broad leaves for latrine hygiene. It was evident that local knowledge and participation needed to be revived, that continuous monitoring of water quality was needed, and that financial incentives would need to be changed to ensure continuous functionality of safe groundwater sources.

The early conversations with the MWE focused on the question: 'Could local technicians be incentivized financially to prevent breakdowns of rural water supply systems?' MWE recognized that rural water systems contained 'gaps': for example, that preventive maintenance had been neglected in practice, if not on paper. MWE was supportive of an organization that suggested solutions to this issue.

Whave Solutions registered as a Ugandan Company with a non-profit resolution in 2012.

2013

In 2013 the Whave Safe Water Security programme started. The programme has two components: building governance collaboratively and service provision. The concept was (and remains) to conduct meetings with local government and MWE in which a system for sustainable assurance of reliable safe water is designed, while at the same time the concept of reliability-oriented performance-payment of local technicians is tested on the ground, providing valuable practical information for the collaborative design process.

By the end of 2013, the results were:

- Just over 100 communities were engaged in trial preventive maintenance services. Eight local technicians were working in those communities under novel performance-paid contracts.
- Continuous monitoring was undertaken of functionality (daily operational reliability of the hand-pumps) and of water quality at source (the hand-pump), as well as in homes (the drinking water pot).
- A series of workshops and meetings brought together stakeholders (local government officials and MWE, HPMAs, and NGOs). These workshops focused on design of a coordinated national system by which all rural communities would have assurance of daily safe water, based on preventive maintenance incentives for local technicians. The participants engaged actively. In smaller meetings, support was given by the Minister and the Commissioner for Rural Water, who took the view that the programme was filling two critical gaps in rural water organization: lack of preventive maintenance and inadequate budget to address a chronic backlog of non-functional water sources waiting for repair and rehabilitation.

2014–2015

During these years a results-based financing solution was developed, centred on reliability-oriented performance payment of local technicians, combined with indicators for sustainability which trigger international aid finance. The intention here was to combine a local solution to a local WASH problem with an international solution to an international WASH problem. The local problem is the perverse incentive of rural mechanics earning from breakdowns rather than from functionality; the international problem is failure to match project funding to sustainability and local economic viability. The local solution was to structure WASH services so that local mechanics earn income from community fees paid for reliable functionality as opposed to earning from breakdowns; the international solution was to design a programmatic budgeting structure centred on paying for evidence of growing reliability and quality of water supply. The same monitoring operation therefore ensured efficient local finance (mechanics' income) as well as efficient international finance. The international results-based financing included tracking a narrowing gap between cost and local tariff revenue, integrated with health and hygiene indicators such as proximity of water supply, adequate volumes consumed, and quality of water at point of use. This approach meant that investors would be paying for audited evidence of progress toward a sustainable WASH solution rather than paying for promises associated with the conventional indicators (e.g. numbers-of-things-paid-for and budget-spend), which in practice hinder sustainable outcomes. A first variation on the results-based WASH system is illustrated in Figure 9.2.

This approach was implemented, and some international financing based on these results was attracted. Considerable evidence was collected showing significant water quality issues in sources and in homes, which revealed several key opportunities for system improvement in the hygiene and sanitation sector. However, in 2016 and after, Whave focused more on reliability of water supply rather than hygiene for two reasons. Firstly, it was evident that reliability assurance starting with hand-pumps was a key step towards investment in piped supply bringing water closer to homes, and proximity of supply was in itself the most effective way of improving hygiene conditions and quality of water in the home. Secondly, the evidence needed for new hygiene interventions was already in place and funding was not yet available to implement the new interventions or further build the evidence base. This last factor was compounded by the fact that a cost recovery strategy could not easily cope with integrated hygiene and water supply reliability; in order to focus on sustainability through cost recovery, it was necessary to focus on reliability.

The diagram shows a revised WASH system suitable for rural piped water as well as hand-pumped water. Local technicians provide preventive maintenance, immediate repair, and 'mobilization', meaning they assist communities to understand and engage in service contracts alongside local government and the service provider. Technicians no longer transact financially with rural community leaders as is the case currently with the community-based maintenance system. Instead a service provider company (Whave is a model service provider (SP) providing on-the-job training to Hand-Pump Mechanics Associations) transacts with community committees (WSCs) who collect tariffs and pay the SP an annual fee. The WSC's role is to ensure poor families have access to water. In this variation of the system model, the WSC saves tariff revenue in a bank account which is supervised by both local government and a local oversight/monitoring body. In a system variation also under development by Whave, the SP directly collects tariff revenue, paying a local collector and sharing it with the WSC. The oversight body monitors hygiene, water quality, reliable functionality (of both piped supply infrastructure and hand-pumps), and financial accountability. It is currently modelled as a public–private partnership collaboration between Whave and local government. The intention is to establish escrow accounts which facilitate coordination of funding sources and stakeholders around a common strategy for self-sustaining effective WASH delivery. This body or partnership is initially established with assistance from aid budgets. These are known as Transfers since monies are transferred from

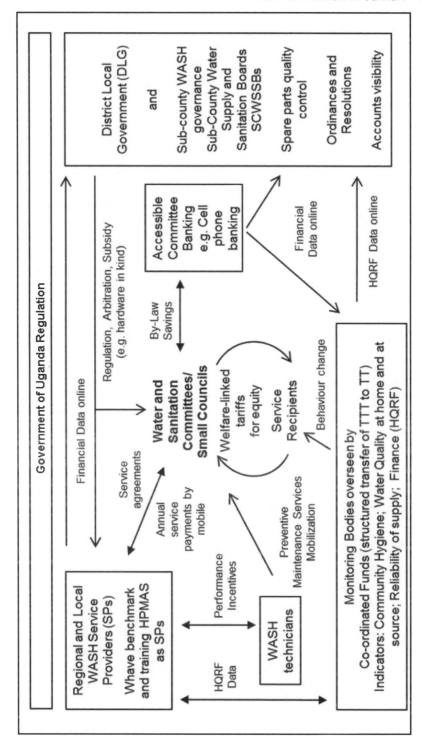

Figure 9.2 Whave system design model

out-of-country sources. The strategy progressively decreases dependence on the Transfers, replacing them with Tariff revenue and government budgets derived from in-country Taxation (Transfer, Tariffs and Taxation (TTT) → Tariffs and Taxation (TT)). In 2018, this process is already under way, with increases in subsidy from government budgets taking place and tariff revenues progressively reducing the role of external aid assistance.

In 2014 and 2015 Whave expanded its practical role as a preventive maintenance service provider and by the end of the period almost 100 communities were signed into fully fledged service agreements, with a consistent record of 99 per cent functionality, compared with a baseline of 60 per cent. Further collaborative design workshops took place with District Water Officers, stakeholders, and MWE, focusing on the challenge of balancing service delivery cost with tariff revenue. It was clear that preventive maintenance was needed and that the performance payment approach was working well, but to ensure it would be self-sustaining, the service company management costs would have to be matched by tariff revenue collected from water users. The necessary tariff rates were estimated at UGX3,000–4,000 (US$0.80–1.00) per family per month. This was recognized as affordable in view of international recommendation of water being within 2 per cent of rural income levels and in view of commercial rates in rural trading centres (typically 10 times more expensive), but the task of collecting sufficient revenue in rural areas was daunting nevertheless. Various models were discussed, in particular the 'individual preventive maintenance service provider' as a low-cost alternative to the regional service provider model. Detailed discussions of pros and cons resulted in a decision, approved by the Commissioner for Rural Water, that the regional service provider model be developed further in preference to an individual model.

2016–2017

The dual approach of consultative design and practical application continued, as it does today. Monitoring continues to play a key role, although more focused on reliability of supply, source water quality, tariff and fee payment compliance, and tracking of cost recovery.

The focus in 2016 and 2017 was the challenge of 'willingness to pay'. The preventive maintenance approach demanded that communities contributed tariff payments before a pump was broken, and this meant placing trust in their community leadership committees and in the technicians visiting their pumps. Trust levels were low in rural Uganda, and it was understandable that families were unwilling to make the necessary pre-payments to committee members and technicians. It was preferable to wait for a pump to fail before considering a cash contribution. This 'wait-till-it-breaks' attitude was compounded by electioneering and NGO presence, because politicians and NGOs often sponsored repairs and rehabilitations of broken and abandoned water pumps.

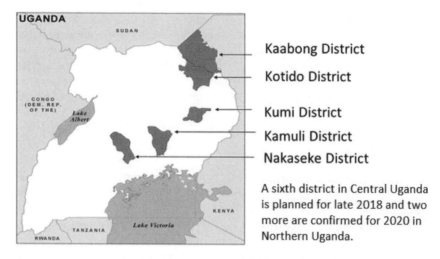

Figure 9.3 Districts in which the public–private partnerships are active in 2018

In the period through 2016 to 2017 the number of preventive maintenance agreements signed with communities grew to over 200, with another 100 in a trial phase, with Whave working as a regional service provider in five districts, as shown in Figure 9.3.

The system worked well in achieving high functionality rates of 99 per cent.

Several collaborative planning workshops took place, leading to the launch of a Safe Water Public–Provider Partnership by a group of districts. The most significant progress in this period was the initiative taken by sub-county councils to pass new legislation. Twelve sub-counties formally resolved that preventive maintenance agreements with an approved service provider were mandatory, and that all rural communities were obliged to elect and register water and sanitation committees as legal entities with publicly supervised bank accounts. This last measure was designed to build consumer trust, since community members could pre-pay tariffs knowing that their committees had legal liability and bank transactions were subject to regular scrutiny. The sub-county resolutions also prescribed minimum tariff amounts, on the principle that committees could diversify tariffs according to welfare needs and so ensure universal access to water, making sure the very poor could still afford tariffs, while larger-volume consumers and businesses would compensate by paying at higher rates.

Throughout this period, all the serviced communities were paying annual fees to the service provider. Fee levels varied from district to district depending on specific conditions. In Kumi, fees rose to UGX350,000 per year per source ($92), while in Kamuli and Nakaseke they rose to UGX250,000 per year per source ($66), since the number of homes sharing one source was lower and therefore individual household contributions were higher.

The collaboration between the prototype service provider, Whave, and the local government, intensified in this period as it became clear that the implementation of the new legislation demanded increasing focus on professional partnership arrangements. Key performance indicators for service delivery were devised, and partnership meetings focused on clear division of roles and responsibilities between communities, the service provider, and local government.

2018 and beyond

Whave's strategy for forthcoming years is focused on achieving financial viability for preventive maintenance services. In 2018 we are preparing a financial model in consultation with local and central government. The plan sets a target for minimized service delivery cost, matched by a tariff revenue and service fee arrangement suitable for communities, combined with government implementation of the regulations recently established.

A key component of the plan is engagement of at least 600 communities in a pilot district. This will involve a social marketing campaign led by local technicians interested in preventive maintenance as an improved professional livelihood. It will be underpinned by the new regulations which require scaled application before they are socially normalized. This market volume is necessary for another reason: to rationalize the management cost of service delivery. Assistance from government with the hardware component of service delivery is under discussion and will help to minimize service fees such that tariffs will be maintained at politically acceptable levels.

Whave will play key roles in establishing the financial viability of service delivery, to create a system that becomes independent of grant funding in several pilot districts within forthcoming years. Economic breakeven is unlikely to be achieved unless 15 to 25 districts are overseen by a regional service provider, with subsidiary local service providers servicing on average 600 communities each. Whave will continue to act as a benchmark or model service provider, demonstrating low-cost management of services which deliver at least 98 per cent functionality. It will also play a second role, continuing as a capacity-building and advisory body for local government. This is an important task, because it creates the regulatory environment which will allow other local entities to become service providers in a coherent market for preventive maintenance services. Local governments will be able to set performance standards, review service provider performance against agreed indicators, and decide service fees and tariffs uniformly through each district. Once these conditions exist, new service providers will be able to build their skills to appropriate levels, obtain licences to operate, and engage with communities on preventive maintenance.

A key role for Whave is therefore the training of local entities to become service providers (see Figure 9.4). Already in early 2018, Whave is partnering with the district HPMAs, to facilitate development of the necessary management

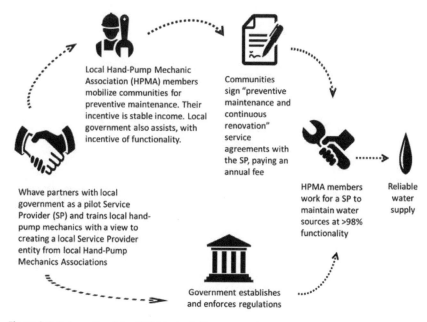

Figure 9.4 Schematic of the WASH adaptation approach

and accounting capacities that the HPMAs will need in order to adopt this role in future years.

Finally, Whave has a key role in working with central government to ensure the pilot partnerships align with national policies and can be replicated at an affordable cost nationally. In the three-year period, Whave will be analysing the feasibility and cost of national scaling in collaboration with MWE. Already plans are in place for expansion from five pilot districts to eight in the period 2018–2020.

About the author

Adam Harvey specializes in rural development in Asia and Africa, particularly in energy and off-grid electricity, fuel-efficient cooking, water access, sanitation, and hygiene. In all sectors, his focus is on rooting solutions in the local economic context, ensuring that local incentives work to build livelihood and environmental improvements permanently. He advises governments on improved regulation and practical public–private partnerships, most recently in the WASH sector. He has an MA from Oxford in Sociology and Economics and a PhD from Warwick University in Engineering, and now lives in Uganda.

CHAPTER 10
Resources for systems thinking

Kate Neely

THIS CHAPTER DESCRIBES SOME of the authors' and reviewers' favourite resources in the field of systems thinking and systems thinking for development. The resources are in no particular order and books, blogs, TED talks, journal papers, reports, and podcasts are all included.

We know that accessing journal papers can be difficult for practitioners. For those of you who have studied at a university, most universities now have a scheme where for a small annual fee any alumni can have access to the library resources, including journals. If you don't have access to university resources, many federal and state libraries have free membership that will grant citizens access to similar resources. Where possible we have included links to free online versions of papers such as preprint repositories or open access journals.

Name of resource:	Type of resource:
Thinking in Systems: A Primer	Book
Author:	**How/where to find it:**
Donella H. Meadows	Wright, D. (ed.) (2008) Chelsea Green Publishing, White River Junction, VT. ISBN 860-1406698703
Why we like it:	
This book is a very approachable place to start your systems thinking journey. It walks through ways to think about systems and problems that can apply to very different parts of our lives. It is also the book that led me to the personal insight that I don't think like everyone else (otherwise the book wouldn't be needed!) and that systems thinking provides a semi-formalized way to explain how I think to others.	

Name of resource:	Type of resource:
'From Poverty to Power'	Blog
Author:	**How/where to find it:**
Duncan Green	http://oxfamblogs.org/fp2p/
Why we like it	
Duncan Green uses and explores systems thinking throughout this blog on topical issues in development. Easy to dip in and out of. The readers of this blog provide really useful comments too.	

http://dx.doi.org/10.3362/9781780447483.010

Name of resource:	Type of resource:
Navigating Complexity in International Development: Facilitating Sustainable Change at Scale	Book
Authors: Danny Burns and Stuart Worsley	Burns, D. and Stuart Worsley, S. (2015) Practical Action Publishing, Rugby, UK. ISBN 978-1-85339-852-0 Available via: http://dx.doi. org/10.3362/9781780448510
Burns and Worsley put a lot of their own development experience under the spotlight to bring us a broad overview of the complex nature of development and development challenges. They don't hesitate to call out poor development practice and constructively work through systems-based approaches that could be used by practitioners, planners, and donors.	

Name of resource:	Type of resource:
A Systems Approach to Modeling Community Development Projects	Book
Author: Bernard Amadei	**How/where to find it:** Amadei, B. (2015) Momentum Press, New York, NY. ISBN 978-1-60650-518-2 <http://www.momentumpress.net/books/systems-approach-modeling-community-development-projects>
Why we like it: Amadei looks specifically at how systems thinking works in a community development context. While focusing on system dynamics, and clearly from an engineering background, this book is a useful reminder of many of the interconnections that we overlook in community development.	

Name of resource:	Type of resource:
How Change Happens	Book
Author: Duncan Green	**How/where to find it:** Green, D. (2016) Oxford University Press, UK. ISBN 978-0-19-878539-2
Why we like it: Duncan Green surveys a myriad of ways that change happens and brings the reader on a journey of discovery based on systems thinking, positive deviance, and other surprising drivers of change.	

Name of resource:	Type of resource:
Understanding Human Ecology: A Systems Approach to Sustainability	Book
Authors:	**How/where to find it:**
Robert Dyball and Barry Newell	Dyball, R. and Newell, B. (2015) London and Routledge, New York, NY. ISBN 978-1-84971-383-2

Why we like it:

Barry Newell is very experienced at teaching people how to use system dynamics and this book offers a clear rationale as it proceeds to teach us how as well as why. The book crosses so many boundaries that it should be essential reading for everyone.

Name of resource:	Type of resource:
NodeXL	Software
Developed by:	**How/where to find it:**
Social Media Research Foundation	https://nodexl.codeplex.com/

Why we like it:

Free and reasonably intuitive software for social network analysis. Works as an add-on to Excel so it's pretty familiar to start with.

Name of resource:	Type of resource:
NetLogo	Software
Designed by:	**How/where to find it:**
Uri Wilensky	https://ccl.northwestern.edu/netlogo/

Why we like it:

NetLogo is a simple, easy to use agent-based modelling software. I wouldn't want to learn by myself but once you get the hang of it, you will want to model everything. Also, you can connect it with a geographic information system and do amazing things with maps.

Name of resource:	Type of resource:
Vensim	Software
Developed by:	**How/where to find it:**
Ventana Systems, Inc	https://vensim.com/vensim-personal-learning-edition/

Why we like it:

Vensim is great for drawing basic influence diagrams and stock and flow simulations. It is easy to use after a little training time and there is a free version for personal and educational users (VensimPLE).

Name of resource:	Type of resource:
'Supporting rights and nurturing networks: the case of the UK Department For International Development (DFID) in Peru'	Book chapter
Authors:	**How/where to find it:**
Fiona Wilson and Rosalind Eyben	Wilson, F. and Eyben, R. (2006), in R. Eyben (ed.), *Relationships for Aid*, Earthscan, UK. ISBN 978-1-84407-280-4
Why we like it:	
Wilson and Eyben take a relationships approach to development that aligns with a systems understanding of effective networks.	

Name of resource:	Type of resource:
Review of the use of 'Theory of Change' in International Development	Report
Author:	**How/where to find it:**
Isabel Vogel for the UK Department For International Development	www.theoryofchange.org/pdf/DFID_ToC_Review_VogelV7.pdf
Why we like it:	
Vogel's approach to theory of change aligns well with systems thinking and incorporates complexity in a practical and enactable way.	

Name of resource:	Type of resource:
Rural Water Supply Network (RWSN) D-group on Complexity and Rural Water Supply	Discussion group
Author:	**How/where to find it:**
RWSN	All discussion topics can be accessed via: www.rural-water-supply.net/en/rwsn-activities/dgroups The discussion on Complexity and Rural WASH can be accessed via: https://dgroups.org/rwsn/rwsn_complexity
Why we like it:	
This discussion group is good because it aims to connect practitioners and researchers with an interest in both systems thinking and WASH. The RWSN D-groups (discussion groups) are a good vehicle for global discussion. This one is underutilized at the time of writing but has the potential to develop a strong following and useful conversations across Systems Thinking and WASH areas.	

Name of resource:	Type of resource:
Guidelines for creating causal loop diagrams	Webpages
Author:	**How/where to find it:**
Daniel Kim, Colleen Lannon, and Kellie Wardman	https://thesystemsthinker.com/ guidelines-for-drawing-causal-loop-diagrams-2/
Why we like it:	
These webpages provide simple tips to get you started on creating a causal loop diagram for your water or sanitation service. These paper-and-pen diagrams can be an effective way of engaging stakeholders on the ground in sharing their perspectives on the important components of a WASH system.	

Name of resource:	Type of resource:
Assessing Resilience in Social-Ecological Systems: Workbook for Practitioners. Version 2.0	Workbook
Author:	**How/where to find it:**
Resilience Alliance	https://www.resalliance.org/files/ ResilienceAssessmentV2_2.pdf
Why we like it:	
This workbook provides more information on social-ecological resilience concepts and templates with instructions for putting the concepts into practice. Designed for practitioners, the activities described in this workbook can be drawn on to inform decision making on how the resilience of WASH services can be enhanced.	

Name of resource:	Type of resource:
Resilience Practice: Building Capacity to Absorb Disturbance and Maintain Function	Book
Author:	**How/where to find it:**
Brian Walker and David Salt	Walker, B. and Salt, D. (2006) Island Press, Washington DC.
	ISBN 978-1-59726-801-1
Why we like it:	
Walker and Salt do an excellent job of explaining and grounding resilience concepts that often feel very abstract to newcomers. Additionally, the authors describe steps and exercises that can be taken to assess the resilience of systems and design interventions for building resilience.	

Name of resource:	Type of resource:
Principles for Building Resilience: Sustaining Ecosystem Services in Social-Ecological Systems	Book
Author:	**How/where to find it:**
Reinette Biggs, Maja Schlüter, and Michael Schoon (eds)	Biggs, R., Schlüter, M., and Schoon, M. (eds) (2015) Cambridge University Press, Cambridge. ISBN 978-1-10708-265-6 A summary is available at: www.stockholmresilience.org/research/research-news/2015-02-19-applying-resilience-thinking.html

Why we like it:

This book walks the reader through resilience principles, describing in detail how they actually build resilience of social-ecological systems and providing empirical evidence. The book also usefully highlights gaps in our current understanding about resilience.

Name of resource:	Type of resource:
Shit Flow Diagrams	Website
Author:	**How/where to find it:**
Sustainable Sanitation Alliance	http://sfd.susana.org/

Why we like it:

Shit flow diagrams (SFDs) are a useful tool for understanding and visualizing how excreta physically flows through a city or town. This website allows you to generate your own SFD, which can be used to help create a system map of a sanitation service.

Name of resource:	Type of resource:
Social Network Analysis: Methods and Applications	Book
Author:	**How/where to find it:**
Stanley Wasserman and Katherine Faust	Wasserman, S. and Faust, K. (1994) Cambridge University Press, Cambridge. ISBN 0-521-38707-8

Why we like it:

This book is a comprehensive introduction to the use of social network analysis, incorporating theory, instruction, and examples. It manages to be an enjoyable read at the same time.

Name of resource:	Type of resource:
Social Network Analysis: A Handbook	Book
Author:	**How/where to find it:**
John Scott	Scott, J. (2017) Sage Publications, London.
	ISBN 978-1-47395-212-6
Why we like it:	
A concise introduction to applying social network analysis.	

Name of resource:	Type of resource:
Governing the Commons	Book
Author:	**How/where to find it:**
Elinor Ostrom	Ostrom, E. (2015) Cambridge University Press, Cambridge.
	ISBN 978-1-10756-978-2
Why we like it:	
Ostrom's approach to understanding common pool resources and their governance via collective action is rigorous and full of examples of both success and failure. It is not easy, but is definitely worthwhile to read.	

Name of resource:	Type of resource:
'Places to intervene in a system'	Journal paper
Author:	**How/where to find it:**
Donella Meadows	*Whole Earth*, Winter 1997 or
	http://donellameadows.org/wp-content/userfiles/Leverage_Points.pdf
Why we like it:	
This document discusses how and when intervention in a complex system can be useful. It is a worthwhile read for anyone who wants to see change in the systems they live and work within.	

Name of resource:	Type of resource:
'Systems thinking and practise for action research'	Journal paper
Author:	**How/where to find it:**
Ray Ison	Chapter 9 of Reason & Bradbury *The SAGE Handbook of Action Research*, also at http://oro.open.ac.uk/10576/
Why we like it:	
As WASH researchers, we are generally predisposed to action research. Ison discusses the history of different forms of systems thinking and action research. The paper highlights ways to think with systems within an action research paradigm.	

Name of resource:	Type of resource:
'Puppies! Now that I've got your attention, complexity theory'	TED talk
Author:	**How/where to find it:**
Nicholas Perony	https://www.ted.com/talks/nicolas_perony_puppies_now_that_i_ve_got_your_attention_complexity_theory#t-730918
Why we like it:	
Great introduction to how the emergence of complex systems occurs based on simple rules. Also sometimes we need puppies and meerkats!	

Name of resource:	Type of resource:
'Is life really that complex?'	TED talk
Author:	**How/where to find it:**
Hannah Fry	https://www.ted.com/talks/hannah_fry_is_life_really_that_complex
Why we like it:	
Takes us on a short journey that explains social modelling (and leopards' spots).	

Name of resource:	Type of resource:
'The implications of complexity for development'	Blog
Author:	**How/where to find it:**
Owen Barder	https://www.owen.org/blog
Why we like it:	
Owen Barder is a development economist who regularly takes a complexity lens to development. Use the search bar for 'complexity' from inside the blog.	

Index

Page numbers in **bold** refer to tables and in *italics* refer to figures.